Exiting the Extraordinary

Exiting the Extraordinary

Returning to the Ordinary World after War, Prison, and Other Extraordinary Experiences

Frances V. Moulder

LEXINGTON BOOKS
Lanham • Boulder • New York • London

Published by Lexington Books
An imprint of The Rowman & Littlefield Publishing Group, Inc.
4501 Forbes Boulevard, Suite 200, Lanham, Maryland 20706
www.rowman.com

Unit A, Whitacre Mews, 26-34 Stannary Street, London SE11 4AB

British Library Cataloguing in Publication Information Available

Library of Congress Cataloging-in-Publication Data

Moulder, Frances V. (Frances Valentine), 1945– author.
Exiting the extraordinary : returning to the ordinary world after war, prison, and other extraordinary experiences / Frances V. Moulder.
p. cm.
Includes bibliographical references and index.
ISBN 978-1-4985-2019-5 (cloth : alk. paper) – ISBN 978-1-4985-2020-1 (ebook)
1. Life change events. 2. Adjustment (Psychology) I. Title.
BF637.L53M68 2016
155.2'4–dc23
2015031381

Printed in the United States of America

Contents

Preface   vii

Introduction   xi

Part I: Extraordinary Experiences   **1**
1   Some Extraordinary Experiences   3
2   Why People are Transformed by Extraordinary Experiences   23

Part II: Returning to the Ordinary World   **49**
3   Contexts of Return   51
4   The Challenges of Returning to the Ordinary World   69
5   Strategies for Returning to the Ordinary World   93
6   Implications for Public Policy   119

Appendix A: Methodological   137

Appendix B: Theoretical   139

References   145

Index   151

About the Author   155

Preface

I began writing this book in the past decade; however, I started thinking about the topic long ago. Some people who were important to me in my earlier years told me stories about extraordinary experiences they had gone through. The stories they told me, and the way they told their stories, made me curious about people who had done things that others are not likely to do, and about what it is like to return to the ordinary world after that.

The first person was my mother. My mother, Rebecca Moulder, had been an aspiring journalist during the 1930s, first in Memphis, then in Washington D.C., and New York City. She had moved in circles in which people were passionate about the issues of the day—birth control, class and racial inequality, the rise of Fascism, and the merits of Capitalism vs. Socialism and Communism. At the end of the decade, she returned to her hometown of Knoxville, Tennessee, where she met my father and settled into an ordinary, domestic life, interrupted only by their involvement for a few years in the Civil Rights Movement. When my mother confided in me about her past life, which was often, there was always a tinge of regretful nostalgia. I was puzzled by the salience her past life seemed to have to her, although I grew accustomed to it. I was a little unsettled by her seeming rejection of the only world I knew.

I encountered the second person when I went away to college in the 1960s. Frederick W. (Fritz) Henssler was my first sociology teacher, an emigrant from Germany. He told me that as a young man, he had been a member of a leftist group in Germany that was active in opposing the rise of Fascism. This was not the Communist Party, but an anarcho-syndicalist group, which was critical of the Soviet Union, and in favor of worker democracy. Its philosophy was actually quite similar to the emerging U.S. New Left's ideas about "participatory democracy." When the Nazis began round-ing up leftists, Fritz narrowly escaped capture, hiked out of Germany to Switzerland, then made his way to Cuba and Argentina, and finally the U.S., arriving in the early days of the Cold War and the peak of anti-Communism. When I met him, he was leading a quiet life as a teacher and researcher, and his life seemed to center around his work. He rarely spoke about his past. My college years coincided with the Civil Rights Movement, growing opposition to the Vietnam War, and the rise of the Student Movement and the New Left. I was surprised when my mentor discouraged me from getting involved with New Left activities of the time, since these seemed to me to be so consistent with his own political ideas. I did not understand why his past life seemed so disconnected from his present life.

I went on to become a sociologist and a college professor. Then my life took a different path. In the later 1970s, I took some time off from the Ivory Tower and spent a number of years as a community educator and organizer. I worked in low income communities and lived in poverty, a milieu very different from the academic world I had found myself in for most of my adulthood. When I returned to the academic world, I was baffled to find myself more out of place than I had expected. I struggled to connect my past with my present. As a sociologist, I recognized that I was going through a cultural transition; however, when I asked myself what to do about it, there were no clear options. I was busy preparing classes, so I put my questions on the back burner.

As it happened, after I returned to teaching, I eventually began teaching at a community college. At Three Rivers Community College, I found myself encountering students with past lives. Some had been in prison, the military, and unusual religious groups; some had been 9/11 first responders. In a setting full of first generation college students, and a growing number of immigrants from Asia, Africa, and Latin America, the students with extraordinary pasts were even more "non-traditional" than most. I also began to learn about some of the extraordinary places in the local community; I took students on visits to a local minimum security prison, where we would meet with a group of prisoners to discuss their lives in and out of prison. I also had students who were corrections officers who shared their insights into the lives of prisoners and the people who work inside prisons.

All of these experiences led me to start thinking about parallels among people who return from what I now call *extraordinary experiences*. Now more settled into my teaching routine, I began to look for sociological studies of the phenomenon. I discovered that this was a topic that sociologists had not fully explored, and I decided to research and write about it. In 2004 I was granted a sabbatical leave to study anti-racism and intercultural communication programs. My project was to develop a multicultural education initiative for our increasingly diverse college population. This project helped me to see the phenomenon of *exiting the extraordinary* in a larger cultural context.

Some researchers use insights from their own life narrative to inform their research ("autoethnography"). Except for the subjectivity in my initial questioning, I have sought to achieve as much objectivity as possible. This book is based on my research rather than on my own life. I have, however, been gratified to find myself beginning to answer the questions I have wondered about throughout my life. I will be pleased if the book also resonates with others who have had similar questions.

I would like to thank the many people who helped me along the way as I worked to write this book. I especially thank the people who shared with me their stories of extraordinary experiences and return to the ordinary world. Most asked to remain anonymous, so that except for Anita Schorr, I do not name them here. I was enlightened, inspired, encouraged, and humbled by everyone I interviewed. Some of them also read a draft of the manuscript and gave me feedback, for which I am doubly grateful. I also thank the writers of memoirs, autobiographies, biographies, and other works about extraordinary experiences that I refer to throughout the book. I am deeply grateful for the information and insights provided by these authors. I am very indebted to all the people who reviewed the manuscript in various versions and made countless invaluable suggestions: the members of my writers group at the University of Connecticut—Ruth Glasser, Kristina Gibson, and Anne Gebelein—my husband Peter Anderheggen, my stepdaughter Shanti Anderheggen, also Cecile Emond, Katherine Holmsen, Kathy Norris, Sandra Norris, Marilyn Ottone, Hope Payson, Mary Schindewolf, JoAnn Smith, and Luther Wilson. Special thanks are owed retired editor Luther Wilson, without whose guidance this book probably would never have been published. I also appreciate the encouragement of: Zoe Anderheggen, George Anderheggen, Margaret Dillon, Anne Doyle, David Emond, Jennifer Gero, Seth Kershner, Gloria Lawton, Norman Norris, Michelle Pouliot, Minati Roychoudhuri, Debra Sargent, Audrey Solnit, Quentin Schaffer, and Stephen White. I would also like to acknowledge the encouragement and support I received from all my colleagues at the University of Connecticut, especially the faculty and staff of the Torrington Campus, the Litchfield County Writers Project, and the Urban and Community Studies Program. I also appreciate the encouragement and support I received from my students, especially Jessica Colin-Greene. I was greatly assisted and guided by University of Connecticut Torrington Campus librarians Sheila Lafferty and Diane Mather who answered my questions about databases and patiently helped me as I checked out hundreds of books. I hugely appreciate the advice and support of my editors at Lexington Press: Brighid Stone, Joseph Parry, Lara Graham, and Sarah Craig. They patiently answered my many questions and helped me "dot every 'i' and cross every 't'" until this book made its way into print. I am especially grateful as well to the anonymous reviewer who made numerous helpful comments and criticisms. I am sure there are many others working at Lexington Books whose names are unknown to me, but who have had a hand in making the book happen, from professionals to service and production workers, and I wish to acknowledge them as well. Of course, none of these people are responsible for any flaws in the book; those are entirely of my own making.

Introduction

EXITING THE EXTRAORDINARY

Some people have experiences in life that are so *extraordinary* that they cannot at all be adequately explained to those who have not had such experiences. Experiences of this sort include: being in military combat; participating in great social movements, revolutions, or terrorist activities; being incarcerated in concentration camps, the *Gulag*, and prisons; surviving collective disasters such as hurricanes or floods; serving in intelligence agencies and undercover roles; being a member of unusual religious groups; working as a journalist in war zones; carrying out aid work in impoverished or war-torn regions; and enduring slavery. This book is about people who exit from these kinds of experiences and return to an ordinary life. As diverse as the experiences just listed may seem, they have some important common characteristics, which will be described in chapter 1. Above all, they are experiences that happen within groups with distinct cultures, and that have great political, moral, historical, or spiritual meaning to their participants. Many people who return to the ordinary world after an extraordinary experience of this sort feel that they have been forever changed by the experience. They feel there is a great gap between themselves and others who have never left the ordinary world. Many face a variety of difficulties in returning to the ordinary world. Although millions of people in the modern world have returned from extraordinary experiences, there is not much social support for those who struggle during the process of returning. Many even exit extraordinary experiences, only to find that their ordinary world is gone, obliterated by war or disaster; they endeavor to resume an ordinary life in an unfamiliar milieu. While some returnees grow and thrive after their extraordinary experiences, it is not unusual for returnees to live lives that are deeply trying and unfulfilling.

Charlotte Delbo, who was imprisoned in Auschwitz for her resistance activities in occupied France, wrote a poignant essay, "Thirst," which captures the essence of the gulf between those who have had extraordinary experiences and the people in everyday life who have not had those experiences. She describes in excruciating detail her memories of an extreme thirst she endured for several days in Auschwitz. Delbo was

> thirsty to the point of losing my mind, to the point of being unable to eat because there was no saliva in my mouth; so thirsty I couldn't speak because you're unable to speak when there's no saliva in your mouth. My parched lips were splitting, my gums swollen, my tongue a piece of wood. My swollen gums and tongue kept me from closing my mouth, which stayed open, like that of a madwoman with dilated pupils in her haggard eyes.

She survived only because comrades managed to sneak a pail of water to her, when they were out on a work detail. Delbo "knelt near the pail and drank like a horse . . . plunging my whole face." Delbo contrasts this thirst with the way thirst is experienced by people in ordinary life: "There are people who say, 'I'm thirsty.' They step into a cafe and order a beer." (Delbo 1995:142–45)

PURPOSE OF THIS BOOK

The purpose of this book is to explore the *commonalities* among extraordinary experiences and the process of returning from them. As far as I know, this book is the first study of such *commonalities*. Other scholars have studied particular examples of extraordinary experiences or the process of returning. For example, there are bodies of literature on the return of veterans, prisoners, child soldiers, and *Gulag* survivors. Practitioners such as social workers, psychotherapists, and advocates also work with particular types of returnees. To my knowledge, however, the commonalities among extraordinary experiences and the process of returning have received little attention. Yet these commonalities are striking, once one pays attention to them. When I first began working on this book, my primary interest was in exploring the process of *returning*. But I soon realized that in order to understand the process of returning, I would also have to define what I mean by extraordinary experiences and explain why participants return to the ordinary world so changed by them. Thus the book's purpose became twofold: to explore the commonalities among extraordinary experiences, and the process of returning from them.

WHY STUDY THIS TOPIC?

Why should we try to understand the common nature of extraordinary experiences and the process of returning to the ordinary world? The perspective of sociology and other social sciences is that culture and society shape how individuals think, feel, and act. Thus sociologists have sought to understand the effect on human behavior of general social structures, such as social class, race/ethnicity, and gender, organizations, and institutions; and general social processes, such as bureaucratization, growing technological complexity, globalization, modernization, or the development of the capitalist world system. This perspective, which C. Wright Mills called the *sociological imagination*, helps us see that problems which at first glance seem to be problems of individuals, may have their origins in larger social-historical patterns, and require public action if they are to be fully solved. I believe that from a sociological perspective, having an extraordinary experience and returning from it shapes a person's life, much as a life is shaped by other social structures and processes. I contend that understanding this point can benefit both individuals and societies. Individuals struggling with the process of returning from extraordinary experiences can benefit from seeing their own personal situations within broader social and historical contexts. Societies will be better able to handle problems related to returnees from extraordinary experiences if their members understand these as public issues everyone has some responsibility for, rather than the personal problems of troubled individuals.

The topic has great contemporary relevance. Although it is not a new phenomenon for people to return to an ordinary world after extraordinary experiences, the phenomenon is more prevalent today and seems to be growing. Humankind has a long history of warfare, imprisonment, disasters, slavery, social movements, and revolutions. For millennia, traders, pilgrims, and migrants have left home for unfamiliar lands. Surely the Europeans who took part in the Crusades of the eleventh to the thirteenth centuries, or the Chinese traders of the Ming Dynasty fleets that traveled around the world must have had challenges if and when they returned to an everyday life. However, people who had exited from the extraordinary would have been a rarity in most communities. In earlier times *most* people were hunter-gatherers or peasants rooted to ordinary lives in particular cultures. Those who went away rarely returned home, since transportation was inconvenient, slow, and costly. Wars or plagues were suffered by entire communities; people did not return to an ordinary world of others who had *not* been affected.

Recent centuries have been times of great growth in the numbers, both absolute and relative, of people who have gone through extraordinary experiences, and returned to an ordinary world. The rise of the capitalist world system, the modern nation-state, and globalization have resulted in massive transformations in the personal life histories of countless individuals. Consider the twentieth century: around the world, millions of people returned home from extraordinary experiences in two World Wars and other major conflicts (e.g., Korean War, War in Vietnam); genocides (e.g., the Holocaust, Rwanda); revolutions, both successful and unsuccessful (e.g., in Russia, China, South Africa, countries in Central and South America); and large scale social movements (e.g., unionization, civil rights, peace, students, feminism, LGBT rights, environmentalism). The twenty-first century appears to be continuing this trend—wars in Iraq, Afghanistan, Africa; genocidal conflicts in Sudan; mass shootings in the U.S. and other nations; revolutions and civil wars in the Middle East, incarceration on a large scale in the United States; and a growing list of natural and socially created disasters (hurricanes, tornadoes, tsunamis, floods, nuclear meltdowns, etc.).

The public is not well informed about returnees, and misconceptions and contradictory views abound. For example, some people may expect a returnee to be the same person they were before they left, like the vacationer who returns with new trinkets and some interesting stories but is otherwise unchanged. Others may expect that a returnee will inevitably be suffering from Post-Traumatic Stress Disorder (PTSD) or other psychological problems. Some may think that such a returnee needs medical help. Others may believe that the returnee can or should just "suck it up" and go on as though the experience had never happened. Some people may feel free to ask a returnee all sorts of intimate questions about the extraordinary experience ("did you kill anyone?" "were you brainwashed?"). Others may avoid the topic out of lack of curiosity or because they think that the topic is too uncomfortable, none of their business, or that the returnee will not want to talk.

What is the impact on societies of such large numbers of people facing the struggles of returning to an ordinary life? Will extraordinary become the new ordinary? Perhaps it is not accidental that we are beginning to see for the first time the emergence and growth of programs and institutions dedicated to helping people successfully navigate a return. Perhaps the worldwide development of programs to help military veterans, child soldiers, civilian survivors of wars/genocides, and the formerly incarcerated reflects a growing awareness that exiting the extraordinary, at least in some circumstances, is a social issue that should concern us all, rather than simply a private or personal issue of individuals.

WHO SHOULD READ THIS BOOK?

I have written this book for several audiences. First, I believe the book will be of interest to academic readers in sociology and other social sciences. The book explores an important topic in a new way. Academic readers include students, and I have endeavored to write in a style that will be accessible to college undergraduates, so that the book can be used as a supplemental reading in relevant courses. Second, I hope the book will help those exiting the extraordinary to see their situations in a broader perspective, and navigate their struggles more successfully. Third, I hope the book will bring greater clarity to families, friends, and others who seek to provide support to returnees, such as therapists, social workers, or medical personnel. Fourth, I also anticipate that the book will enable others who have experienced any sort of time period away from the ordinary, to get insight into their lives. There is a spectrum of experiences from the most mundane to the most extraordinary, and surely there is a fine line between the extraordinary and others that are perhaps less extraordinary, but still unusual. Finally, I hope that the general reader will find the book enlightening, and consider answering its call to support changes in interpersonal behavior and public policy to ease the struggles of those who exit the extraordinary.

RESEARCH DESIGN AND METHODOLOGY

This book is an *exploratory* study. *Exploratory research* looks into a previously unstudied topic and seeks to generate an initial understanding of the topic (Babbie 1992: 90–91). As mentioned above, there is a body of research on some categories of extraordinary experiences and returnees, but not on the commonalities among them. I began without a preconceived theory or hypothesis. Instead, I looked into sources of information about these sorts of experiences and the process of returning, and drew comparisons among them as they revealed themselves to me. I cast a wide net in terms of the scope of the study. Although I was limited to English language sources, I included experiences from around the world. I also included experiences from recent historical times as well as the present.

I used a variety of research methods. I looked first to sources that would give me the perspective of participants. I began by reading memoirs, autobiographies, oral histories, and biographies of people who had gone through extraordinary experiences and returned to a more ordinary life, looking for commonalities among the experiences as well as the process of returning. Using library search engines, I developed a reading list of works in each category of experience, for example, works by or about Holocaust survivors, combat veterans, former prisoners, etc. Some of these were monographs, e.g., memoirs or biographies about one person's experience, others were compilations, such as edited collections of shorter memoirs or biographies, or scholarly accounts of interviews with a number of people. One of my first disappointments was finding that the memoirs, autobiographies, oral histories, and biographies tend to cover the extraordinary experiences at length, but say relatively little about the return process. I tried to focus my reading as much as possible on works that dealt with both aspects.

At a certain point in my reading, I was able to arrive at some generalizations about commonalities among extraordinary experiences and the return process, and although I continued reading, further reading did not seem to be giving me major new insights. I wondered whether the generalizations uncovered through the reading would also emerge using a different research method. I decided to supplement the reading with some confidential interviews. I interviewed nine people who had gone through one or another type of extraordinary experiences. This included three veterans of the wars in Iraq and Afghanistan, two child survivors of the Holocaust, an undercover police agent, an aid worker with experience in war zones in Africa and Asia, a former soldier in World War II, and a woman who had been a Roman Catholic nun in the 1960s before the Church liberalized practices in its religious orders. I located the interview subjects through my professional networks and friends. I told everyone about my research and asked them to refer me to people I might interview. I also asked interviewees to refer me to other people I might interview. This process had some drawbacks. It resulted in a narrow sample. I was not able to find people to interview in every category of experience. And the interviewees are by and large middle class and European-American. However, I did find that the interviews supported and enhanced the generalizations I had been developing through the broader reading, which gave me more confidence that these generalizations might be reasonable. At the point when additional interviews did not seem to be yielding any major new insights, I concluded this phase of the research.

Throughout the time I was reading and doing interviews, I was also reading a variety of *secondary sources*. I read books written by scholars who had researched and analyzed specific categories of experience. These helped fill in gaps in my knowledge that arose when I could not find many writings by or about individuals in certain categories of experience, or when I could not locate interview subjects in certain categories of experiences. At the same time, I also read more theoretical work in sociology and other social sciences, in an effort to make sense out of the research findings. There are two bodies of theoretical literature I found most useful: studies of self and identity, and studies on social roles and "role exit."

First, literature about how the self has been interpreted in the fields of sociology, anthropology, social psychology, and intercultural communication. Studies of the self in relation to culture are rich with insights about self and identity in the context of nation, class, ethnic group, and gender. Returnees from extraordinary experiences are not unlike the "marginal" people who inhabit the study of identity in cross cultural transitions—for example, people who emigrate from their homeland to a foreign country, or who climb from a lower to a higher status in the hierarchy of social class. I am much indebted to this field of study.

The second is the sociological literature on social roles and "role exit." There is a great deal of sociological theory and research into social roles, the self, and identity. Helen Ebaugh's pioneering research, *Becoming an Ex* (1988), examined the situations of people exiting such varied roles as doctor or lawyer, nun or priest, spouse, man or woman (gender changes), and prisoner. Ebaugh found that people who are deciding to exit from roles go through typical stages, no matter how different the roles. In the final stage, which is the most relevant for this book, they leave the role and go on to face a number of challenges as they construct an identity or sense of self, which is new, yet typically encompasses the "ex" role ("ex-con," "divorcee," etc.) (Ebaugh 1988:149–80). I am much indebted to Ebaugh's research, and that of others who followed in her footsteps, especially for the idea of the "ex," and the idea that people face a variety of challenges as they reconstruct their identity. I have diverged from this body of knowledge, however, in that I believe that the concept of "role" is a bit too narrow to encompass either the nature of extraordinary experiences, or the challenges that follow exiting from them. Also, I have not investigated why and how people decide to exit from extraordinary experiences, in order to devote more attention to how people manage their lives *after* their exit.

Strengths and Limitations of the Research Design

One strength of exploratory research is that it uncovers new insights. I believe that taking a broad and open-ended perspective has enabled me to generate some new insights into both extraordinary experiences and the return process. The social sciences today have become more and more specialized, to the point that sometimes we know more and more about less and less, missing the forest for the trees. This book has taken on a very large topic and while some may find its vision overly broad, others may find it a refreshing reminder of what is important about the social sciences.

Another strength of exploratory research is that it can shed some light on available research methods for studying the topic. Perhaps my exploration of sources will be helpful to future researchers. Until I examined memoirs, autobiographies, etc., I had no way of knowing how useful they would be. As mentioned above, I did not initially plan to do interviews, but in the course of time, I decided they would be a useful supplement to the written sources. It seems clear to me now that although there is a wealth of material available in the form of memoirs, oral histories, autobiographies, and biographies, it is uneven, in the sense that these works were written to fulfill certain purposes of their authors, which may or may not mesh with the goals of the researcher. As noted above, there is not as much coverage of the return process as there is of the extraordinary experiences. Moreover, there is less information about some categories of experience. For example, there are more memoirs, oral histories, autobiographies, and biographies about military veterans and Holocaust survivors, and not as many about returning undercover agents, aid workers, social movement participants, disaster survivors, and former members of unusual religious groups. Perhaps other researchers who are concerned with broader comparative questions will consider moving directly to interviews or taking approaches entirely different from mine.

Exploratory research is not without limitations. Just as an explorer of an unknown geographic terrain may map its general features but not the details, I have not asked and answered every question that could be addressed. For example, there are of course differences among extraordinary experiences, but I have not tried to examine all of these differences in detail, or to describe their consequences for returnees and the return process. This is an interesting and important question, but for the most part the sources I found did not contain enough information on this point to justify making generalizations about it. (There is one exception—the consequences of having had an extraordinary experience that is highly *stigmatized* by members of society.) However, taking lemons and making lemonade, at relevant junctures in the book I bring up unasked and/or unanswered questions and encourage readers to be inspired to do further research into these topics.

Also, in my quest to map the general terrain, I may have missed some of its features that would be obvious to a different researcher. Although I made an effort to find authoritative secondary works by scholars on various categories of experience, I may have overlooked important works since I am not an expert in every area. Readers who are specialists in certain fields may find I have missed works they think are important, and suggest revisions to my generalizations. Finally, although I have sought to attain a broad historical and global perspective, there is some emphasis on the United States. This is partly because I limited my sources to works in the English language, but also because as an American citizen, I hope to have some impact on my fellow citizens' thinking about our nation's public policies. International readers may believe that I have omitted important material, and suggest revisions that may be needed.

OVERVIEW OF THE BOOK

Part I of the book is about what I discovered regarding the nature of extraordinary experiences, as necessary background to understanding the process of return. It seeks to answer two questions: *What are extraordinary experiences? Why are people often so profoundly altered by going through such experiences?* Chapter 1 focuses on defining what I mean by extraordinary experiences and illustrating my definition with examples from my research. In this chapter I create a model of the characteristics of extraordinary experiences, a kind of *ideal type*. The *ideal type* is an intellectual approach developed by sociologist Max Weber, in which one distills from many examples those characteristics that seem most essential for understanding the nature of the phenomenon. (In Weber's usage, the term "ideal" means a logical conception, not an evaluation or judgment.) I then present seven stories of extraordinary experiences drawn from memoirs which illustrate the characteristics of such experiences, envisioned as an ideal type. Chapter 2 is an analysis of how these characteristics of extraordinary experiences help explain the mystery of why individuals are often so profoundly changed by them, rather than being like the vacationer who returns with the new trinkets and some interesting stories. It brings together theoretical concepts from the social sciences with more examples from my research.

Part II covers what I learned about the process of return. It explores five key questions: *What are some of the social contexts to which people return? What challenges do returnees face? What are some strategies returnees have used to try to meet these challenges? Can any of these strategies help a returnee become happy or satisfied in the ordinary world? How can societies support returnees more effectively?* Each chapter in part II contains many examples from my research. Chapter 3 is about the typical social contexts faced by returnees, some of them positive, some negative, and some ambivalent. It covers family contexts as well as overall societal contexts. Chapter 4 is an overview of typical personal challenges faced by returnees, ranging from material survival to more intimate issues concerning the self and identity. Chapter 5 is about typical strategies that are pursued by individuals as they seek to deal with these challenges. Some of these seem to be more effective than others in promoting individual satisfaction or happiness with life in the ordinary world, and I make an analysis of why this is so. The conclusion is about public policy. I make some recommendations and provide some examples of existing initiatives that seem to promote greater satisfaction or happiness among returnees.

The book also contains two appendixes, one methodological, one theoretical. I decided to cover certain matters in appendices rather than footnotes, in order that students and general readers would find the book more readable. In the Methodological Appendix, I provide more information on my interview process, including the interview format and a summary list of interviewees with the pseudonyms I have given them. In the Theoretical Appendix, I cover certain conceptual and theoretical questions that may be of interest, such as the meaning of "ordinary world," why I have used certain types of experiences, and not others, to develop my *ideal type* definition of extraordinary experiences, and why I have chosen to use certain social science concepts in my analysis, and not others.

Part I

Extraordinary Experiences

Chapter One

Some Extraordinary Experiences

What are extraordinary experiences? In this chapter, I outline the essential characteristics of extraordinary experiences as an *ideal type*, and present, as illustration, seven stories of extraordinary experiences drawn from memoirs. This chapter is background to the next, in which I look at the question: *Why are people so profoundly altered by going through extraordinary experiences?*

EXTRAORDINARY EXPERIENCES: AN IDEAL TYPE

As mentioned in the introduction, I am using an *ideal type* approach to defining extraordinary experiences. An ideal type is an intellectual model of a phenomenon made for the purpose of analysis. It is not simply a summary of all the characteristics possessed by every specific example of the phenomenon. Instead, it is a list of the characteristics that seem to the analyst to be *most important for an understanding* of the phenomenon. For example, Max Weber's model of *bureaucracy* includes characteristics such as fixed and official jurisdictional areas; rules and regulations; a hierarchy of authority; specialized and salaried jobs requiring expert training; and impersonality (Gerth and Mills 1946:59–60, 196–239). Weber compared bureaucracy, so defined, to other forms of organization prevalent in earlier times, such as *feudal* structures, which had very different characteristics. Not every bureaucracy in the modern world has all the characteristics in Weber's ideal type. But by knowing the characteristics in Weber's concept, one can get insights into how bureaucracies often operate. I have created a model of extraordinary experiences for the purpose of understanding how these experiences compare and contrast with those in the ordinary world, and why people are changed by going through them. There may be some specific extraordinary experiences that lack one or another of the characteristics in my model. But I believe that the model helps us understand how extraordinary experiences often operate.

Extraordinary experiences as an ideal type have three major characteristics: first, the experiences happen within a group or collectivity, which has a common culture that is very distinct from the mainstream; second, the experiences have great political, moral, historical, or spiritual significance or meaning to the participants, a meaning which is very different from the meaning of life in the ordinary world; and third, the experiences, even if harsh, contain moments or events in which participants feel joy, happiness, pride, excitement, or other positive emotions.

Extraordinary experiences *happen within a group or collectivity*, rather than being experiences of isolated individuals. In the vocabulary of the social sciences, extraordinary experiences happen within distinct *cultures.* Participants inhabit a cultural world which is so different from what people in the mainstream culture are accustomed to, they might as well be from another country, or another period of history. They have learned and lived by a distinct set of values, norms, beliefs about reality, technologies, styles of communication, and languages or dialects. As a result, their sense of self and identity changes; they are no longer the person they were before the experience and have instead become a person adapted to the extraordinary culture, a topic to which I will return in the next chapter.

Second, these are cultures that convey to participants *a sense of great political, moral, historical, or spiritual significance*, which may result in participants not only changing but changing deeply, even becoming wrapped up in their new self and identity. There is a deep sense of self connected with the extraordinary experience that is very different from the more distant way that people in the ordinary world tend to relate to their identities as workers, family members, or participants in recreational groups, a topic to which I will also return in the next chapter. Participants in extraordinary experiences often see themselves as making history, saving the world (or their own particular nation, ethnic group, or social class), enduring unique hardships, uncovering the truth, or serving God. The extraordinary culture's norms and beliefs encourage them to see themselves as profoundly different from ordinary people, even superior to them, due to the significance of what they are participating in. We ordinary people may see them in this way as well. As a result, the experience tends to mark a defining rupture with a participant's past (and future) identity, something that forever divides a personal history into "before" and "after."

A third and final common characteristic of extraordinary experiences is that even in the harshest settings participants may experience times of *positive emotions*, such as satisfaction, happiness, excitement, or joy, even if fleeting—times of pride in accomplishment, of taking comfort from familiar routines, of resting at the end of a hard day, of comradeship and community, of loving and being loved, of appreciating beauty. These are not forgotten after the extraordinary experience is over, even when people in the ordinary world (and perhaps the returnee, as well) expect the returnee to have "moved on." Not all extraordinary experiences are unrelievedly negative, unpleasant, dangerous, or "traumatic" (life shattering or life threatening). Some are, but some are just the opposite. For example, taking part in a great social movement, carrying out aid work, or patriotically identifying with an undercover role may be experienced as nothing other than a series of positive challenges and opportunities for personal growth. However, even participants in extremely negative experiences report occasions of positive feelings; that these are found in the shadow of hardship and the threat of injury or death, may make them all the more hard won and precious.

I arrived at this ideal type by examining experiences in the categories listed in the Introduction—military combat; great social movements, revolutions or terrorist activities; incarceration in concentration camps, the *Gulag* and prisons; collective disasters; intelligence agencies and undercover roles; unusual religious groups; journalists in war zones; aid workers in impoverished or war torn regions; and slavery. There are other experiences the reader may think of as "extraordinary" and wonder why I did not examine them in order to arrive at the ideal type. In the Theoretical Appendix, I explain why I did not include other sorts of unusual experiences, such as being an astronaut, an actor in a long-running musical, a gang member, or a member of Congress. For the most part, they were omitted because in order to highlight what it is about extraordinary experiences that makes them so life altering, and makes the return to the ordinary world such a struggle, I created a model drawn from the more *extreme* examples. In doing so, I believe that I manage to clarify more fully the problems of returning to the ordinary world, than I would otherwise have been able to do. I believe we can get to the issues of the actor in a long-running musical returning to an everyday life by first understanding the problems of the child soldier returning to school; the other way around does not work as well. This is because in the extreme cases, we see a greater number of the dimensions involved, and we see them with the greatest clarity. Please see the Theoretical Appendix for further discussion of this point. There I also explain why I omitted experiences undergone by individuals alone (e.g., a believer in alien abduction), and experiences manufactured for profit (e.g., "reality" television programs or wilderness adventures).

SEVEN EXTRAORDINARY EXPERIENCES

Some examples of extraordinary experiences can help bring to life the essential characteristics just described. In the remainder of the chapter, I present the stories of seven people who went through extraordinary experiences. At first glance, the experiences may seem quite different—they include an inmate in a concentration camp, two participants in the Civil Rights Movement, a soldier in the U.S. Marines, a survivor of an airplane crash, an African child soldier, and a war correspondent. But if we look more closely, they share the essential characteristics of extraordinary experiences: each of them happened within collectivities that constituted distinct cultures; they had great political, moral, historical, or spiritual significance to the participants; and they contained aspects or moments of positive emotions.

A NAZI CONCENTRATION CAMP SURVIVOR

The story of Primo Levi, a Jewish-Italian survivor of Auschwitz, illustrates all the characteristics of extraordinary experiences, but it especially highlights the distinct and unusual culture of the concentration camp. Levi was by profession a chemist, but in my view he was also a social scientist. His writings display keen observational skills and insightful sociological imagination. His description of the culture of Auschwitz is, in my estimation, unparalleled.

Levi wrote about his experiences there: "I remember with a certain relief that I once tried to give courage . . . to an eighteen year old Italian who had just arrived. . . . But I also remember, with disquiet, that when I had been in the camp for almost a year. . . I had deeply assimilated the principle rule of the place which made it mandatory that you take care of yourself first of all" (Levi 1988). Inmates of the Nazi concentration camps were treated with a systematic cruelty that is hard to comprehend. There were thousands of these camps, large and small, imprisoning people from groups the Nazis had targeted as scapegoats for persecution and/or annihilation—Jews, leftists, the disabled, Roma, homosexuals, and Christian religious minorities such as Jehovah's Witnesses. Prisoners of war, and laborers taken from occupied territories were also forced into camps. As a processing center for prisoners who were eventually sent to other camps, Auschwitz was an experience many victims of the Nazis had in common. Levi's memoir, *Survival in Auschwitz* (1985), and his more analytical book, *The Drowned and the Saved* (1988), provide detailed descriptions of the culture of Auschwitz and reveal the shock, astonishment, and bewildered horror felt by inmates when they first stepped into the camp and became subjected to its order.

Born in 1919, Levi came from a stable middle class family, and grew up in Turin. As a youth, he was an excellent student who loved to read and showed a scientist's and engineer's talent for building and experimenting. Although often in poor health, he enjoyed skiing and hiking. His education was marred by bullying and anti-Semitism in schools and university, but he graduated with a degree in chemistry from the University of Turin. After graduation, he managed to find employment, even as Fascists were taking over Italy. In 1943, Levi joined a group of anti-Fascist young people that took to the mountains. Unfortunately, they were naive and were soon infiltrated by an informer who betrayed them. Levi had not been participating very long when the group was discovered and arrested (Angier 2002; Thomson 2002).

Although Levi had already endured several days of transit to Auschwitz in a train without food, water, heat, sanitary facilities, or sleeping accommodations, the first encounter with Auschwitz still amazed him. Entry into the camp involved a series of frightful and humiliating rituals. Imagine that you have arrived with Levi at Auschwitz. People arrived there—Levi, young Jewish mothers with children, entire extended families, schoolboys and schoolgirls, carpenters, professionals. They may have arrived with a suitcase containing belongings—clean clothes, valuables, toiletries. They were accustomed to a life of law and order, respect and comfort. First, as soon as they got off the train, SS men ordered family members to separate—men from women and children. People came and took away all their belongings. Then, SS men separated those who looked fit to work for the war effort from the sick, feeble, and old, who were taken away to be gassed and cremated (Levi 1985:20).

The soon-to-be workers were led to places where SS men ordered them to strip naked, shower in harsh disinfectants, dress in prisoner rags, and put on broken, badly fitting wooden shoes, all the while compelling them to run at full speed from one processing station to the next. An official tattooed each man's arm with a number. Finally, they were marched to barracks, where hundreds would sleep, two to a bunk, on filthy straw mattresses, each with a dirty blanket. Levi describes his bewilderment and astonishment with every step of the processing. In the first stage, he and the other men were waiting in a huge, cold empty room, terribly thirsty. There was a water tap and above it a sign: "it is forbidden to drink the water as the water is dirty." Levi thought this had to be some kind of cruel joke (Levi 1985:22). Later, the SS men tell them to take their shoes off and put them in a corner. A man swept all of their shoes into a pile outside the room. Levi thought it was crazy to separate the pairs this way (Levi 1985:23). After the showers and head shaving, the prisoners look at one another: "for the first time we became aware that our language lacked words to express this offence, the demolition of a man. In a moment . . . the reality was revealed to us: we had reached the bottom . . . no human condition is more miserable than this, nor could it conceivably be so" (Levi 1985:26–27).

After the entry processing rituals, prisoners began their new life, ordered around by SS officers or by underlings recruited from the inmate population. It was common for SS men, or underlings, to beat them, often for arbitrary reasons, which served to intimidate. The inmates were fed only thin soup and a small amount of bread, despite working extreme hours at back-breaking labor. There was a humiliating and painful daily roll call ritual, during which inmates were forced to stand for hours on end, exposed to the elements, depending on the season, hot sun, or freezing rain or snow. Those who could not stand were selected out, and taken away to be killed. Levi learned a host of "incredibly complicated" rules:

> the prohibitions are innumerable—to approach nearer to the barbed wire than 100 yards; to sleep with one's jacket, or without one's pants, or with one's cap on one's head; to leave the hut with one's jacket unbuttoned, or with the collar raised. . . . The rites to be carried out were infinite and senseless: every morning one had to make the "bed" perfectly flat and smooth; smear one's muddy and repellant wooden shoes with the appropriate machine grease; scrape the mudstains off one's clothes (paint, grease, and rust stains were, however, permitted) . . . (Levi 1985:33–34).

One of the most shocking things to Levi was how dead human bodies were treated. The treatment of

> those remains, which every civilization, beginning with remotest prehistory, has respected, honored, and sometimes feared . . . was intended to declare that these were not human remains, but indifferent brute matter, in the best of cases good for some industrial use. . . . Human ashes coming from the Crematorium . . . were employed . . . as fill for swamp lands, as thermal insulation between the walls of wooden buildings, and as phosphate for fertilizer; and especially notable, they were used instead of gravel to cover the paths of the SS village located next to the camp (Levi 1988:125).

Despite this daily routine of horror that threatened to annihilate them, and the constant presence of death, many prisoners in the camps also made an effort to hold on to the humanity and decency of their former way of life. They helped one another, shared food and clothing, listened to storytellers, held religious rituals, planned resistance activities, and engaged in musical and artistic activities. Those who could sew became tailors for the others; there was an informal market, in which inmates who had become traders organized the exchange of soup, bread, tobacco, spoons, shirts, and all sorts of items pilfered from the workplaces or infirmaries. Life was not without some joys. The ghastly circumstances, however, also promoted the rise of a predatory culture. Levi wrote that inmates stole from one another—food, soup spoons, fabric to stuff into the soles of their broken shoes. Many were also willing to cooperate with the Nazis. It was a key path to survival to become one of the so-called "prominents" of the camp—prisoners became "Kapos" (Directors), cooks, nurses, night guards, sweepers, kettle washers, latrine and shower monitors. Prisoners were even commandeered to run the Crematorium (Levi 1988:50).

The struggle to endure in the concentration camps held moral and spiritual significance for many. In regard to the Jewish people, Lucy Dawidowicz, in *The War against the Jews*, points out that there is an "exceptional responsibility that traditional Judaism places on every Jew. The obligations to preserve Judaism and the Jewish people rested not on monarchs or prime ministers, nor on high priests, prophets and rabbis, but on each Jewish man and Jewish woman." This "prime value that the Jews attached to life itself and to Jewish survival resulted in an activist tradition" (Dawidowicz 1986:342). The experience of Isaac Bash, a Hungarian Jew who survived the Golleschau camp is described as follows by Bernice Lerner in *The Triumph of Wounded Souls.* "Ever aware that the suffering inflicted upon him was part of a heinous plan to annihilate the Jewish people, Isaac prayed not for himself alone. When he fought to save his own life, he fought a larger battle. If he survived, the Jewish people had a chance of being ensured. Being wholly directed toward an entity beyond himself gave Isaac's life meaning . . . Isaac's reason to live was both personal and communal" (2004:34–35). He wrote later, "my being a religious Jew has helped me a great deal to recover. I have always believed in *Netzach Yisroel,* the eternity of the Jewish people. And that was more important to me than my own well being or success" (Lerner 2004:35). To Primo Levi, a more secular person, the significance was not simply spiritual and moral, but deeply political. His desire to write about his experiences to expose the Nazi cruelties, was an inherent and ongoing part of his struggle to live through the ordeal. "My need to tell the story was so strong in the camp that I had begun describing my experiences on the spot, in that German laboratory laden with freezing cold, the war, and vigilant eyes." Levi described his need to tell the story "an immediate and violent impulse, to the point of competing with our other elementary needs" (Levi 1985:9). He was too frightened to keep his notes, and threw them away. "Nevertheless these memoirs burned so intensely inside me that I felt compelled to write as soon as I returned to Italy" (Levi1985:375). Levi attributed his survival not only to luck, but also to his "interest, which has never flagged, in the human spirit and by the will not only to survive (which was common to many) but to survive with the precise purpose of recounting the things we had witnessed and endured" (Levi 1985:397).

Levi's extraordinary experience of Auschwitz ended in January of 1945, as the Russian army drew near. The Germans fled, and days later the camp was liberated by the Russians.

A SOLDIER IN VIETNAM

In his best-selling book, *Born on the Fourth of July,* Ron Kovic described his childhood, and his experiences in the Marines during the War in Vietnam, including boot camp, combat, and his return home as a paraplegic (Kovic 1976). Kovic's story illustrates all of the characteristics of extraordinary experiences, but especially demonstrates the great significance or meaning participants attach to the experiences. Kovic was drawn to the Marines because military service had a special political and moral significance to him. As he encountered the realities of the war in Vietnam, he began to see the politics of military service in a very different light, and became an anti-war activist.

Kovic was 18 and just out of high school in 1964 when he followed a childhood dream and joined the Marines, eager to respond to President John F. Kennedy's appeal to serve his country. He had grown up in Massapequa, New York. It was a quiet and stable life, full of routines. As a child, Kovic played baseball, watched the Yankees on television, and went to the Catholic Church on Sundays. At the same time, from school and television, he absorbed the national passion against Communism, and followed with fascination the U.S. efforts to catch up to the Soviet Union in the space race. He went with friends to see war movies at the local cinema, and the boys played war games in the woods with machine guns and pistols. Kovic's Dad worked as a checker at the A & P, and Kovic "didn't want to be like my Dad, coming home from the A & P every night. He was a strong man, a good man, but . . . it took all the energy out of him. I didn't want to be like that, working in that stinking A & P, six days a week, twelve hours a day. I wanted to be somebody" (Kovic 1976:60). In high school Kovic excelled on the wrestling team, and at track and pole vaulting. He delighted in his growing athletic prowess, and formulated the desire to "be a hero." And when recruiters from the Marines visited the high school, talking about building men and serving the country, Kovic began thinking about joining. He signed up the summer after graduation (Kovic 1976:60–61).

Kovic endured boot camp with a determination to succeed at his dream of being a soldier-hero in the fight against Communism, but also with dismay and a strong desire to escape. On the first day, drill sergeants shouted at the men, cursed and demeaned them. Other men shaved the heads of the recruits, and made them strip and shower in a batch. Their civilian clothes were taken away, and a sergeant screamed orders at them to get dressed in poorly fitted uniforms. He bullied an overweight boy who could not fit into the pants that were given him. Then they were made to run, in the heat, carrying heavy bags with clothing, until many could not keep up and began to crawl (Kovic 1976:72–73). Kovic captured his mixture of fear and determination in a stream of consciousness style:

EYES RIGHT! I WANT YOU TO BELIEVE THIS AFTERNOON THAT THIS THING OUT THERE IS A COMMIE SONOFABITCH *and wops and spics and chinks and japs and GET IN FRONT OF YOUR RACKS!! THAT'S NOT QUICK ENOUGH! (never quick enough, eighteen i'm eighteen now)* UP! DOWN! GET IT! OUT! GET IT! *oh mom o please o someone someone help now somebody* . . . YOU BETTER BE DEAD IF YOU DROP OUT . . . FORWARD MARCH! *oh mary mother of jesus you gotta help me* . . . *oh get me outta here god* . . . (Kovic 1976:76,78)

Kovic was sent to Vietnam, became a sergeant, and served two tours. Expecting to fight the Communist enemy, his first two combat experiences instead involved him in the wrongful deaths of a fellow soldier, and innocent Vietnamese civilians, which left him with unresolved feelings of guilt and confusion. In the first case, a young corporal was shot and killed during a confusing firefight. Kovic thought he had done it, but was not absolutely sure. Even though he confessed this to a major, he was either not believed, or excused, and there was no punishment. He never even discussed it with anyone else, although he sensed that other soldiers might be talking about him behind his back. In the second case, he and fellow soldiers fired repeatedly into a peasant hut where they thought enemy soldiers were hiding, but it turned out that the hut contained only one old man, whose brains had been blown out, and many severely wounded children. Kovic and others helped the children, as best they could, bandaging wounds and calling for a helicopter to evacuate them (Kovic 1976:191–193).

After the civilian deaths, Kovic felt terrible (Kovic 1976:194). Other narratives about Vietnam contain similar references to American soldiers reacting this way to the culture of impunity and lawlessness that came to characterize the war. In addition to civilians being tortured and killed—by the allied South Vietnamese troops, by the Viet Cong, by Americans—prostitution and drugs were pervasive, and American soldiers were ordered by their superiors to fabricate the "body counts" that were used to document America's progress towards victory. Young American draftees were haunted by knowing that American youth from wealthier families were receiving draft deferments. They were disturbed when they went on leave in Saigon, and saw young Vietnamese males enjoying a carefree civilian life (Polner 1971: 24, 51–52, 71–72, 80–85).

After the civilian deaths, Kovic experienced many dangerous patrols, suffering with guilt, and still hoping to fight the enemy rather than friends. But he also began to wish he would be wounded, so he would be sent home. He began to take risks. Finally, in an assault on a village, Kovic fought the enemy and received the wounds that did send him home. At first he was shot in the foot. Despite his injury, he kept on firing, heedless of what might happen to him, and then was very seriously wounded (Kovic 1976:195, 205).

Kovic's war experience continued after he was returned to the U.S. and entered a Department of Veterans Affairs (VA) hospital that treated the badly wounded. "The hospital is like the whole war all over again" (Kovic 1976:29). Every third day, the men were placed in frames in order to be given an enema, in a row, as though they were in an assembly line. Kovic wrote, "This is a nightmare" (Kovic 1976:24). The men were also showered in their frames "like a big car wash" (Kovic 1976:25). Back in their rooms, others could look in and see them "through the curtains that never close. It is as if we are a bunch of cattle, as if we do not count any more" (Kovic 1976:25). The wards were dirty, and there were rats. The hospital was understaffed with uncaring workers, so that men got bedsores from not being turned enough. "Urine bags are constantly overflowing onto the floors while the aides play poker on the toilet bowls in the enema room . . . it never makes any sense to us how the government can keep asking for money for weapons and leave us lying in our own filth" (Kovic 1976:28).

Kovic's extraordinary war experience ended when he was discharged from the hospital and sent home to live with his parents again in his childhood home, now equipped with a wooden wheelchair ramp.

A CHILD SOLDIER IN SIERRA LEONE

Extraordinary experiences are by no means confined to adults. Children have been soldiers in many wars in recent history, in countries as diverse as Sierra Leone, Afghanistan, Uganda, Angola, Liberia, Cambodia, Myanmar, Mozambique, Guatemala, Honduras, Sri Lanka, and Chechnya. A memoir by Ishmael Beah tells the story of his extraordinary experiences as a child soldier in the government army during the civil war in Sierra Leone in the 1990s (Beah 2007). In the unusual military culture he was forced to join, adult soldiers provided children with a rationale and the skills for killing. Even though a child, Beah found clear moral and political meaning in his experiences and also had positive feelings about some aspects of his service.

Beah was twelve years old in 1993 when the village he had grown up in was attacked by rebel forces fighting the government. Until this time, Beah had a peaceful childhood. His father worked for a foreign corporation, and Beah often went swimming in a pool and watched television at the place where foreign workers lived. Although his parents' marriage had ended, and he had to quit school because his father had stopped paying for it, he spent time with both parents, enjoyed a relationship with a loving grandmother, and was close to his older brother. Because his mother was not at home with him, he felt like a misfit in the village, but he did not suffer for lack of food or clothing, and he dressed in fashionable Western baggy jeans and shirts. He passed his days dancing and singing in a rap group with other boys. The boys were free to play and wander about; they swam in the rivers, and enjoyed boyish activities like using a slingshot to chase monkeys and shoot at birds (Beah 2007:6–11).

At the time his village was attacked, Beah was away in a neighboring town. He had gone there with other boys to take part in a talent show. Separated from his family, Beah fled in the company of other boys, including his brother, walking a long distance to try to get to a safe zone. Beah was hungry, and worried about his family (Beah 2007:17). The boys survived by helping one another and strategizing how they might endure. They first returned to the town in the hopes of finding some money they had left behind. The town was an awful sight, with objects scattered everywhere and corpses out in the open (Beah 2007:23–27).

Beah wandered for months, enduring other horrifying events, and was eventually captured by government forces and forced to become a soldier for the government. Captured boys were given army clothes, sneakers, AK 47s, and ammunition, put through basic training exercises, and taught how to use and clean the weapons. Some of the boys were so little they could barely lift the guns up to fire them; the guns were taller than they were. In the training exercises, they were made to stab banana trees with bayonets (Beah 2007:109–113). A corporal yelled at them: "Visualize the banana tree as the enemy, the rebels who killed your parents, your family, and those who are responsible for everything that happened to you . . . this is how I do it. I first stab him in the stomach, then the neck, then his heart, and I will cut it out, show it to him, and then pluck his eyes out. Remember, he probably killed your parents" (Beah 2007:112). The boys became very angry as they adopted this point of view. Soon they were taken into combat. Before going, they took tablets of some sort of drug they were told would give them more energy (Beah 2007:116). When the fighting began, at first, Beah was extremely frightened and could not shoot. Then he witnessed the death of two boys who had been his close companions. "Suddenly, as if someone was shooting them inside my brain, all the massacres I had seen . . . began flashing in my head. Every time I stopped shooting to change magazines and saw my two young lifeless friends, I angrily pointed my gun into the swamp and killed more people" (Beah 2007:119).

Beah became accustomed to the routine of a government soldier. In the daytime, he stood guard, smoked marijuana, sniffed a concoction of cocaine mixed with gunpowder, and took the tablets, which he had become addicted to. At night, the soldiers watched *Rambo* movies, or raided rebel camps and civilian villages, to capture recruits and supplies. The adult soldiers taught the boys that they were defending their country against rebels who killed for no reason. The boys were made to kill rebel prisoners (Beah 2007:121–25). "I felt special because I was part of something that took me seriously, and I was not running from anyone anymore" (Beah 2007:124). "My squad was my family, my gun was my provider and protector, and my rule was to kill or be killed. The extent of my thoughts didn't go much beyond that. We had been fighting for over two years and killing had become a daily activity. I felt no pity for anyone . . . it seemed as if my heart had frozen" (Beah 2007:126).

Beah's extraordinary experience ended in 1996, when boy soldiers were demobilized and taken by United Nations personnel to a rehabilitation center where they would made a transition back to civilian life (Beah 2007:128–137). He eventually came to the U.S. and began a new life path, starting with high school.

A WAR CORRESPONDENT

Chris Hedges was for many years a war correspondent for the *New York Times* and other newspapers. "War and conflict," he has written, "have marked most of my adult life." He reported on insurgencies in El Salvador, Guatemala, Nicaragua, and Colombia. He covered the first *intifada* in the West Bank and Gaza; civil war in Sudan and Yemen; the Gulf War, the Kurdish rebellion in southeast Turkey and northern Iraq; Bosnia and Kosovo; and other conflicts in North Africa, Eastern Europe, and South Asia (Hedges 2002:2).

War correspondents share many of the same extraordinary experiences as combatants and civilians in a war zone, although they may go back to a hotel room to file a report to their newspaper or news service. Hedges wrote a reflective book on war, *War is a Force That Gives Us Meaning*. His account shows a deep grasp of the impact of culture on the individual, and insight into the political, moral, and spiritual significance many people find in war. Hedges also describes the positive emotions he felt when in war zones, even though his life was often in danger.

As he reported on war, Hedges felt both horror and an intense sense of excitement and purpose. He experienced this early in his career in El Salvador. He covered a firefight in the Salvadorean town of Suchitoto, which had been surrounded by rebels of the Farabundo Marti National Liberation Front, during a period in which the rebels were winning the war. It was a very dangerous place and several reporters had already been killed there. Hedges and other reporters entered the town from the outskirts, along with the rebel fighters, and got caught in the midst of a firefight between the rebels and the soldiers of the defending garrison. Diving for cover, he heard wounded and dying rebels calling out in pain. Full of adrenalin, his heart racing, he managed to escape to safety (Hedges 2002: 42). But as time passed, Hedges came to accept the thought that he would die in El Salvador. He had to leave the country three times because he received tips that death squads planned to kill him. Yet he returned again and again, as he found that being in a war zone was more attractive than returning to the "routine of life" (Hedges 2002:5). Hedges wrote of war: "The enduring attraction of war is this: Even with its destruction and carnage, it can give us what we long for in life. It can give us purpose, meaning, a reason for living. Only when we are in the midst of conflict does the shallowness and vapidness of much of the rest of our lives become apparent. . . . And war is an enticing elixir. It gives us resolve, a cause. It allows us to be noble" (Hedges 2002:3).

Hedges came to see war as kind of a "twilight zone," it was so extraordinarily different from what a human being usually expects from life. In a small Albanian village in Kosovo, he covered scenes of villagers identifying the bodies of their slaughtered relatives. He pulled back cloths covering faces, recorded the mutilation of the bodies, watched as relatives sobbingly tried vainly to wash away bloodstains from faces (Hedges 2002:75). Journalists in war zones confront this "twilight zone" over and over. In Kuwait, after the Gulf War, Hedges witnessed scenes of carnage in a seven mile line of Iraqi vehicles that had been strafed by fighter jets. His senses were assaulted by the sight of charred bodies still inside cars, trucks and tanks, and the smells of rotting corpses. In the Kurdish safe area of northern Iraq after the war, he watched while gravediggers unearthed the remains of 1,500 soldiers who were said to have been shot after refusing to fight in the 1980s war with Iran, and when Kurds identified the remains of loved ones killed by the Iraqi secret police. He read records, and saw photos and videos of secret police executions; he visited former torture chambers. Hedges witnessed children who had been shot by soldiers in El Salvador, Guatemala, Sarajevo, and Algeria, and in Gaza, he visited a refugee camp next to which Israeli soldiers were taunting children over loudspeakers, and shooting them when they ran close to throw rocks (Hedges 2002:85, 136–40, 93–94).

Hedges' career as a journalist in war zones ended in 1998, when he left the Balkans to study at Harvard and attain a Master of Divinity degree. He has continued as a writer and is also an activist in progressive causes. An interview with Hedges can be found in a contemporary documentary, *Under Fire: The Psychological Costs of War Reporting* (Burke 2011).

TWO CIVIL RIGHTS WORKERS

The Civil Rights Movement of the 1960s provided experiences to participants equally as extraordinary as the concentration camp and war experiences just described. The next stories are of two young women, one African American, one white, who both participated in the Civil Rights Movement in and around Albany, Georgia. The stories especially illustrate the enormous moral and spiritual significance this movement conveyed to its participants. We also get a glimpse of the special culture of the Civil Rights Movement, and the positive emotions felt by participants, despite the stress and fear that they often suffered. The first story is of Janie Culbreth Rambeau, a young African American college student in Albany, Georgia at the time the Student Nonviolent Coordinating Committee (SNCC) came to the area; the second is of Penny Patch, a young white college student from the North who was the first white woman to work in a Southern field project of SNCC.

The Civil Rights Movement in the early 1960s was based on the idea of the Beloved Community, as taught by Reverend Martin Luther King, Jr. and other organizers such as Jim Lawson. John Lewis describes the meaning of the Beloved Community in his memoir, *Walking With the Wind,* as he learned it from Jim Lawson of the Fellowship of Reconciliation during non-violence training Lewis participated in when he was a young student at the American Baptist Theological Seminary in Nashville, Tennessee:

> According to this concept, all human existence throughout history . . . has strived toward community, toward coming together . . . Wherever it is inter-rupted or delayed by forces that would resist it—by evil or hatred, by greed, by the lust for power, by the need for revenge—believers in the Beloved Commu-nity insist that it is the moral responsibility of men and women with soul force, people of good will, to respond and to struggle nonviolently against the forces that stand between a society and the harmony it naturally seeks. This was eye-opening stuff for me, learning that the feelings I'd had as a boy, the exclusion and unfairness that I had witnessed growing up in Alabama, the awful segrega-tion that surrounded all of us here in Nashville and throughout the south— throughout the entire nation—was nothing new . . . These were incredibly powerful ideas, and their beauty was that they applied to real life, to the specifics of the world we walked in (Lewis 1998:78–79).

Janie Culbreth Rambeau had grown up in segregated Albany, Georgia. As a child, she heard many stories of cruelties to African Americans, and experi-enced prejudice herself. Her awareness and intolerance of injustice increased over time, and she knew that many people felt the same way she did—as she has described it, "there was an accumulation." When organizers from SNCC came to town to organize protests, she and others were eager to take part (Rambeau 2012:91–93). In 1961, Rambeau participated in the first large march, and was among the many people arrested and put into overcrowded jail cells. The cells were damp and cold, and dirty, with the water fountains located over the toilets. But participants endured jail as a special and impor-tant experience—they saw themselves as challenging the *fear* upon which the South's entire system of white supremacy was based. The system of white supremacy depended on African Americans being fearful: fearful of going to jail, fearful of beatings, fearful of lynching, fearful of losing one's job, one's home, of being thrown out of college. The mass arrests and jailings that followed protests during the Civil Rights Movement helped break that fear.

People went to jail, proudly and willingly, singing songs of defiance (Rambeau 2012:93–95).

Rambeau was a student at Albany State College at the time, and was expelled from the college as a result of her involvement in the march. She was not alone; others were also expelled from Albany State, and this fate was shared by other Southern college students who took part in the Movement. Rambeau then began to work on another aspect of the organizing, a voter registration drive. She and other organizers went from house to house in an effort to persuade African American people to register. This was not easily accomplished. Many were afraid, or unable to share the vision of the Movement that voting could actually bring about change. Whites spread rumors that people's Social Security or pensions would be cut off if they registered. "Sometimes there'd be a thunderstorm and because we were from the Movement, people wouldn't let us shelter on their porches." The Albany Movement was met with violent repression. People were hurt when they were thrown into jail and taken to court. An African American attorney, C.B. King, was attacked by a sheriff when he went to a local jail to represent a white SNCC organizer. At a protest outside a jail, a woman, Marion King, who was six months pregnant, had a miscarriage after she was kicked by a policeman. Five homes of people involved in the voter registration campaign were shot at (Lewis 1998:185,191).

Rambeau has described herself as "called" by the Movement; she was thrilled by its spirit. The marches and mass meetings were especially moving. The mass meetings included speeches and singing, and they gave participants a "boldness, that calling . . . after those meetings we were ready to go anywhere and do anything. Some people say we got closer to the Lord during the Movement. I do know we got closer to one another, thereby getting closer to God . . . there was fire in our singing: those songs touched you way down inside until you shook." She was also drawn by the diversity of participants in the marches—students, "people of every color," many religions, ministers—"just the idea of seeing that many people hand in hand sends chills up and down my spine" (Rambeau 2012: 96, 99).

Rambeau eventually returned to college to complete her undergraduate degree, and also earned several master's degrees and two doctorates. She became a teacher and a Baptist minister (Rambeau 2012: 99–100).

Penny Patch's father had worked for the U.S. Foreign Service, and Patch spent much of her 1940s and 1950s childhood in other countries, including China, Czechoslovakia, and Germany. Her parents were very interested in political issues and had strongly held opinions, including the idea that everyone has a responsibility to make positive contributions to changing the world. As a child, Patch had thought deeply about the question of why Germans had stood by during the Nazi persecutions. At the age of fifteen, the family returned to the U.S. and although Patch had never had much contact with

African Americans, when she learned about the problem of racial segrega-
tion, she wanted to do something about it (Curry et al. 2000:134–38).

After high school in New York City, Patch went to Swarthmore College
in Pennsylvania, a college influenced by Quaker values and principles. She
soon became involved with student groups from both African American and
white colleges which were organizing sit-ins at segregated restaurants on the
Eastern Shore of Maryland. She has described this movement as "electrify-
ing." "I can remember the headiness of those days, the sense that we were
doing something important and that we were doing it together, black and
white" (Curry et al. 2000:139). As a result of Patch's activism, at the end of
her first year in college, she was invited by Charles Sherrod of SNCC to join
the voter registration project in the rural counties around Albany, Georgia.
Patch first worked in Albany, living with a local African American family.
She and other organizers canvassed door to door in the African American
community, encouraging people to register to vote and to attend the mass
meetings (Curry et al. 2000:142–43). After a month or so, Patch was trans-
ferred to a rural county, north of Albany, which had been plantation country.
Again, she took part in door to door canvasses, urging people to register to
vote and to come to local meetings or meetings in Albany (Curry et al.
2000:145–46).

Due to the ever present possibility of violent retaliation, the Movement,
as described by Patch, had many rules designed to protect its participants.
Women were not allowed to wear pants because Southern rural African
American women did not wear pants. Participants were forbidden to drink
alcohol, because this was not approved of in the Southern rural culture, and
could result in arrest. Sexual activity within the staff was not prohibited but it
needed to be discreet, and sexual activity with people not on the staff was
forbidden. Patch was told never to display physical affection for an African
American man in public because it could lead to his being killed. When
SNCC workers traveled in integrated groups, a white person might have to
lie on the floor in the back, covered by a blanket. Despite the fear, participation in the movement remained exhilarating. Patch felt strongly that she was
part of something that held great moral significance (Curry et al. 2000:148).

Patch eventually left the Movement in 1965, when the racial climate
within the Movement began to change. The rise of the Black Power movement had resulted in a growing distance between African Americans and
whites in SNCC, and she no longer felt as welcome as before. She left with
great reluctance and pain (Curry et al. 2000:163).

A DISASTER SURVIVOR

It might not seem that an airplane crash could be an extraordinary experience with the characteristics I have outlined. The idea of culture may imply that there is a history, a permanence of some sort that is not found in a disaster. The harsh and unexpected nature of a disaster might seem to preclude moral or spiritual reasoning, or positive emotions. However, even in disastrous, shorter term experiences, groups of human beings develop culture, and the culture they develop has an impact on the individuals involved. People attach meaning to the experience and find moments of positivity. The following story of Nando Parrado illustrates all of these characteristics of extraordinary experiences.

In 1972, in late winter, a Fairchild twin-engine turboprop carrying forty-five people crashed into a glacier on a mountain slope in the high Chilean Andes. Nando Parrado was a member of a Uruguayan rugby team on that flight. He and his teammates were going to a match in Chile, accompanied by friends, family members, and team supporters. Efforts to find them failed, and rescue attempts were called off. A handful of survivors managed to endure for over two months at an altitude of 12,000 feet. Among them was Parrado, who, with another team member, eventually walked out to civilization across forty-five miles of frozen mountainous terrain, and led rescuers back to the crash site to save the rest of the group (Parrado 2006).

Parrado had been until this point a carefree, young middle class man who had a passion for rugby, sports cars, and girls. His parents owned three hardware stores and the family lived in an elite suburb of Montevideo. The parents had worked their way out of poverty, and provided a comfortable lifestyle for Parrado and his siblings. Seriousness entered Parrado's life primarily in the models of hard work provided by his parents, and in the form of the game of rugby, which he had played since childhood. Parrado had attended a private Catholic school run by the Christian Brothers, who had come to Uruguay from Ireland in the 1950s. The school stressed mastery of the sport of rugby as a way of teaching character and morality—humility, tenacity, discipline, and devotion to others. When Parrado finished school, he began to play rugby professionally (Parrado 2006:7–14, 22, 27).

Thirty-two people survived the crash, mostly young men between the ages of nineteen and twenty-one. The plane's crew had all died except the mechanic. Parrado's mother and sister, who were traveling with him, died, his mother in the crash, and his sister a few days later. The survivors faced horrendous conditions. It was winter, and every night the temperature plunged below zero. They had only a small amount of food, and in the frozen landscape, there was nothing for them to eat. The air was thin, and they faced dehydration in the midst of the snow because they could not melt sufficient quantities of it for drinking (Parrado 2006: 50).

The survivors began to organize themselves almost immediately after the crash, led by the young team captain Marcelo Perez. Medical students within the group tended to the injured. The uninjured boys freed the passengers who were trapped under a heap of wrecked seats. They dragged the dead—as many as they could—out of the fuselage and cockpit and into the open. They cleared floor space within the fuselage to make a place to shelter overnight. They built a wall at the open end out of suitcases, loose seats, pieces of the airplane, and packed open spots with snow. They took the cloth coverings off the seats and used them as blankets. The survivors huddled together the first night, and punched each other's arms and legs to try to keep the blood flowing. The next morning they took down the wall, removed the rest of the dead, and kept working to make a better shelter in what remained of the fuselage and luggage compartment. They gathered all the food they could find and devised a rationing system (Parrado 2006: 54–64).

In the early days after the crash, under Marcelo Perez's leadership, they developed a set of beliefs that helped carry them forward. They became convinced that rescuers were on their way. They also trusted in God and God's goodness. They would say: "God saved us from dying in the crash . . . Why would He do that just to leave us here to die?" Perez argued that they should not ask why God was testing them so cruelly. It was their duty to God, their families, and one another, to accept their suffering and fear and to endure until the rescuers found them. The group prayed nightly for rescue. Parrado and a handful of others were not so sure. After days had passed without any signs of rescuers, they decided to climb higher up the mountain to get a view of the surrounding terrain. They hoped that they would be able to see, beyond the peaks to their west, some glimpse of Chilean lowland. A few of the young men devised snowshoes from seat cushions and climbed higher on the mountain to see what could be seen. After climbing all day in agony, they returned having been unable to see anything except even higher mountains. Parrado was disappointed but did not give up on the idea of escape. Although convinced he would probably die on the mountain, and taking part in the nightly prayers, Parrado made a promise to his father that he would return home to him, and developed a detailed vision of himself climbing first up, and then down the mountains to safety (Parrado 2006:63–69, 77–82).

The group continued to develop an organized way of life. They took turns sitting with the badly injured and comforting them (Parrado 2006:82). They had nightly discussions about history, politics, and religion (Parrado 2006:83–84). Crews were organized to do a daily cleanup of the fuselage and to lay out the seat cushions to sleep on at night. The only woman survivor, the thirty-five year old wife of a male survivor in his thirties, comforted the youngest boys (Parrado 2006:87). When some of the survivors sunk into depression, the others cared for them and prodded them into action without condemning them as they might have before the crash (Parrado 2006:89). One of the survivors devised a way to melt water by using sheets of aluminum found inside the seats. A crew of boys was formed to oversee the melting procedure, and ensure an ongoing water supply (Parrado 2006:92–93). Eventually when the food supply ran out, some recognized that if they wanted to live, they were going to have to eat the bodies of the dead. A meeting was convened and the issue debated. Some argued that God would not forgive them if they did this. One man argued that God would want them to do what was necessary to live. Parrado put forth an idea that caught on: "We must believe it is only meat now . . . The souls are gone" (Parrado 2006:97).

Eventually the group decided to try to get help. Parrado and two of the other stronger men decided to trek out. Parrado described how hard it was to leave the crash site. There were aspects of the experience there that felt positive. He desperately wanted to stay with his friends and continue in the environment that had become "warm and familiar" to him (Parrado 2006:184). After the three men had set out on their mission, they decided that one had to turn back, because they did not have enough food for all three. Parrado and Roberto Canessa hiked for ten days in Mt. Everest-like conditions without any of the sort of protections typically used in extreme hiking. They crossed over a mountain and forty-five miles of mountainous terrain, and eventually encountered some peasants tending their flocks of sheep. The peasants contacted the police, and soon the Chilean air force sent helicopters to fly to the crash site and pick up the other survivors. Parrado was reunited with his father after his extraordinary experience of some seventy-two days (Parrado 2006:183–221, 235 ff.).

I hope that this chapter has begun to answer for the reader the question: *what are extraordinary experiences?* I hope that I have begun to persuade the skeptical reader that despite their diversity, it makes sense to categorize together the experiences of Levi, Kovic, Beah, Hedges, Rambeau, Patch, and Parrado as *extraordinary experiences* having the characteristics of the *ideal type* I have proposed. I also anticipate that the reader has begun to grasp the deep *personal* impact of immersion in extraordinary experiences, with their distinct cultures, significance, and moments of positivity—that it was next to impossible for participants to go through the experience without becoming changed persons, very different from the persons they had been in the ordinary world they had left. In the next chapter, I go further into the question: *Why are people so profoundly altered by going through extraordinary experiences?*

Chapter Two

Why People are Transformed by Extraordinary Experiences

Why are people so profoundly altered by going through extraordinary experiences? In this chapter I explore the answer to this question, bringing together social science concepts with examples from my research. I draw on concepts from my own field of sociology and related fields such as anthropology, psychology, and intercultural communication. (Please note: all of the people I interviewed have been given pseudonyms, with the exception of Anita Schorr, who has become a public figure.)

In the public perception, people who go through extraordinary experiences are changed by the *dramatic events* they face, such as narrowly escaping death, being separated from loved ones, taking part in a historic march, being abused in confinement, or enduring severely harsh conditions. While this may be part of the answer as to why people are so changed, especially in the case of *traumatic* events, it misses another, perhaps more profound point: since extraordinary experiences happen within a distinct culture, participants are being *reshaped* by their overall participation in that *culture*. In chapter 1, I defined extraordinary experiences as happening within a group which has a culture that is distinct from the ordinary world. This point has important implications from a sociological perspective. In sociological perspective, all human beings are creatures of culture: in many ways we think, feel, and act as the cultures we participate in encourage us to do. Thus we might expect that the culture of an extraordinary experience will leave its mark on a person just as the cultures of the ordinary world do, and perhaps even more so, since participants in extraordinary experiences attach such great political, moral, historical, or spiritual significance to what they are going through.

Examples from my research confirm this cultural reshaping in three ways, which I explore in the remainder of this chapter: the occurrence of *culture shock*; changes in participants' sense of *self* and *identity*, and the development of new *habits*. I also discuss *trauma* and its effects on the brain, self and identity. While trauma is closely connected to certain types of *dramatic events,* culture also plays a part, and I elaborate on this point.

CULTURE AND CULTURE SHOCK IN EXTRAORDINARY EXPERIENCES

The Concept of Culture

The presence of *culture shock* is one of the first signs that people in extraordinary experiences are being changed by participating in a different culture, rather than simply by the dramatic events they may be enduring. To explain culture shock, it is important to review the idea of *culture*, as it is understood in sociology and other social sciences. Culture is often defined as the distinct way of life of a social group that is humanly created and passed on from generation to generation, as a way of meeting human needs. Culture is more than just customary practices, like eating with chopsticks or forks. The works of social scientists have illuminated just how much culture governs every realm of human thought, feeling and action. Culture includes the technologies used to survive in the environment; the basic values and norms (morals, laws, rules) people live by; the beliefs they share about reality, including religious beliefs, and the stories they tell about events and the group's history. It includes a group's routines and rituals; their etiquette about social interactions; their styles of communication; their languages, dialects, and accents; their nonverbal language; their notions about which emotions are proper to feel and express; and their understanding of time and space. Culture includes their roles and relationships—mother, worker, student, priest, citizen, ruler, doctor, etc.—and their organizational and institutional forms—family, corporation, medicine, government, education, etc. While human needs may possibly be "universal," or common to all humans, cultures differ in how they structure themselves to meet those needs. Thus for example, while we all need physical or material subsistence, some cultures handle this by hunting and gathering, others use agriculture, and others emphasize manufacturing. While we all need intimacy and sexuality, some cultures handle this by monogamous marriage, others by polygamy, others by polyandry.

We learn our group's culture from others, beginning in childhood. We are constantly influenced to conform to it by systems of *social control* (e.g., rewards and punishments) exercised by others. As a result, for most of us, many of the actions, thoughts, and feelings prescribed by our culture become *habits* of mind and body that we engage in with little conscious thought or reflection. We stop at red lights, keep careful track of our money, watch television, or care for our spouse without very often asking where these behaviors come from. We sense ourselves to be separate beings, or individuals, who even create and change aspects of our culture, and of course we are—but we are also walking, talking manifestations of culture. In this social science view of culture, we are free, but at the same time we are in the grip of culture. As Czikszentmihalyi has pointed out, from the standpoint of culture, individuals can be seen as vehicles through which culture manages to endure over time, just as from the standpoint of human genes, individuals who mate and reproduce can be seen as vehicles for the perpetuation of the genes they carry (Czikszentmihalyi 1993).

The Concept of Culture Shock

Since culture grips us tightly, the experience of leaving our culture for a different one can lead us to feel disoriented and uncomfortable, even depressed. This negative state social scientists call *culture shock* or *transition shock* (Adler 1975; Bennett 1998; Oberg 1960). In the complex and multicultural nations of today's world, most of us transition from one culture to another at some point in our lives, even if we never leave the nation where we were born. When this is anticipated and supported, it can be a relatively easy process. For example, in the course of the life span (e.g., from high school to college, college to career), we often prepare ourselves at one stage for what the next state will bring, a process sociologists term "anticipatory socialization" (Merton 1957). Such life span transitions are often highly structured and assisted (e.g., parents, teachers, mentors, and self-help books teach us what to expect when we become parents or job applicants). However, in other cases, the transition may be harder because support is lacking. For example, social mobility from one social class to another (upward or downward) is usually difficult, as is geographic mobility (rural to urban, or from one region to a very different one).

The difficulty of a transition depends in part on the degree of difference between the culture we are leaving and the one we are entering. Living in a foreign country is a difficult transition that many people make in this era of globalization. Culture shock can be intense because we aren't just observing the other culture from a distance, but are stumbling in our interactions with locals on a daily basis. It is stressful to be amidst others who are living a way of life so different from the one in which we feel comfortable. In a classic analysis of "the stranger," sociologist Alfred Schuetz explained the difficulties of having to interact when first approaching a new group for acceptance. Schuetz used the metaphor of "recipes" to illuminate how cultural knowledge operates. We arrive at the new culture with a set of interpretative "recipes" for understanding the social world that guide how we interact with others. But these recipes derived from our culture of origin do not apply in the new culture, where people operate with a completely different set of recipes. Until we are able to decipher and use these different recipes, we are at a loss (Schuetz 1944). People who study intercultural communication have spelled out a whole host of ways in which we can stumble when we are newcomers to a culture. We haven't mastered the language, so trying to communicate our ideas and needs is frustrating. Nor have we mastered any of the other ingredients of successful social interaction—nonverbal gestures; etiquette in daily activities; rules about how close or how far away to stand to others; knowledge of when touching is or isn't acceptable; and all the differences in values, such as acceptance vs. rejection of power and status inequalities, or individualism vs. a more collective orientation (Ward, Bochner and Furnham 2001:47–69).

Culture shock is not simply the negative state described above. It is generally held to have three stages. The first stage is actually a state of euphoria: excitement and delight at encountering the new experiences. This is followed by the state of disorientation or depression. The final stage is one of adjustment. Culture shock eventually comes to an end. Most people get through the depressed and disoriented stage; they learn how to navigate the new culture's values, norms, and language, and become accustomed to it. Today, the problem of culture shock among travelers is widely recognized and efforts are made to help people anticipate it and deal with it (e.g., by study abroad programs, agencies helping immigrants, corporations, etc.).

Examples of Culture Shock in Extraordinary Experiences

All three stages of culture shock, euphoria, disorientation, adjustment, seem to play out in extraordinary experiences. I found some examples of culture shock when I interviewed two young American veterans about their experiences in Iraq and Afghanistan. Both went through a euphoric period followed by a more negative time, followed by recovery or adjustment. The reader might expect that the depressed state occurred in boot camp, based on the story of Ron Kovic in chapter 1. In fact, it happened later. Cameron Smith, a young Army veteran, had joined the Army Reserves during his junior year in high school and went through basic training during the summer between his junior and senior year. Smith had been full of positive feelings about enlistment. During childhood, he had immersed himself in history, video games, and movies about the military and war. He came to see serving in the military as a "noble cause," a way to help others. He was also influenced by his father, who had himself wanted to join the service and regretted that he had not. In basic training Smith was "the baby." It was a "great accomplishment to keep up with the guys who were older and more fit than I was." He was fascinated to learn about all of the rules and procedures involved in the military. He felt good about having to be responsible, and it was "going backward" when he had to go back to high school after basic training and "be treated like a kid, when the Army treated me like an adult." Smith's euphoric state lasted until his unit was mobilized to active duty, which came after his high school graduation. Sent to Fort Dix for further training, he didn't like it. He didn't know anyone, and felt "angsty." This negative period lasted about three months. But then, his unit was sent to Kuwait, and he began to "perk up. I felt I was in the right place." Later, in Iraq, he took scary patrol duties in stride, and enjoyed many aspects of military life, including learning about Iraqi culture from translators he worked with.

Andres Beaumont, another young soldier I interviewed, is a veteran of the Marines who had been deployed to both Iraq and Afghanistan, and had seen combat in Afghanistan. He too had enlisted with eagerness. As a boy, he had been aware of the attacks on the World Trade Center and Pentagon, and had seen soldiers going to Afghanistan, "I wished I could be there." He wanted to serve his country. Also, influenced by television, movies, and war games, "I wanted to establish myself, show how strong and courageous I was, to prove this to my family." His decision to join the Marines had "an element of bravado." He too was euphoric during boot camp, despite having a fear of failure and punishment. He came home to a "hero's welcome" after boot camp—but like Smith, there was a down period after that when he returned for more training. "No one likes you, you know no one, no one was generally that happy . . . you are the new kid on the block again." Eventually Beaumont gained his wish to be tested in combat, and came to appreciate many aspects of his service.

The concept of culture shock was originally developed in the context of *voluntary* activities, such as international travel for study, work, or tourism, or voluntary emigration, where it is readily understandable that a euphoria stage might precede a stage of depression. Thus it is not surprising that voluntarily chosen extraordinary experiences, such as joining a volunteer military, follow a similar pattern. But one might question whether the stages are the same in an *involuntary* experience—can an *involuntary* extraordinary experience really begin with "euphoria?" My research led me to think that perhaps we should broaden the understanding of the first stage of culture shock beyond "euphoria" into the more general idea that it is a "heightened awareness of self and of one's surroundings." If the experience was *voluntarily* chosen, there is a heightened positive awareness of self and one's environment—great delight and excitement at being in a situation one so greatly identified with and longed for, or euphoria. If entry into the extraordinary experience was *involuntary*, there is also a period of heightened awareness, but it is negative rather than positive, a profound sense of misery at being in a horrific situation one would never have imagined oneself in.

Culture shock in an *involuntary* situation can be seen in the experiences of Primo Levi, whose story was told in chapter 1. In chapter 1, I described Levi's heightened awareness when he first entered the camp, his surprise at the elaborate rituals for dehumanizing the inmates. Subsequently, he seems to have entered the second culture shock stage of depressive confusion and disorientation. After Levi had been at Auschwitz for a week and had not washed himself, a fellow inmate encouraged him to wash. Levi replied that washing took too much energy and they were all going to die anyway. The other prisoner reproached him, saying that washing is an act of resistance, and they would survive if they could force themselves to preserve the habits of civilization. Levi was not convinced, and wondered if it would be better to recognize that one does not know a system for survival that one could have confidence in (Levi 1985:40–41).

Later, Levi pulled out of this state; as we have seen, the desire to one day tell the story was a big part of his resilience and successful survival. Like Levi, most people who endure in an involuntary extraordinary experience seem to eventually get past the period of unhappy disorientation. However, this does not necessarily mean that they "adjust" to the experience in the sense that the international traveler "adjusts" to living abroad or the voluntary enlistee "adjusts" to life in the military. If the experience is involuntary and brutal, a better word might be "endure." I once asked Anita Schorr, a child survivor of the Holocaust, how she had adjusted to Auschwitz. She admonished me: "you never 'adjust' to Auschwitz."

In addition to culture shock, participation in the cultures of extraordinary experiences can result in changes in a person's sense of self and identity. In the next section, I discuss the definitions of *self* and *identity,* and present several other concepts that help explain how self and identity are changed in the cultures of extraordinary experiences: *levels of the cultural self, agency, meaning*, and *engulfment*. Again, I draw on my research for illustrations.

CULTURE, THE SELF, AND IDENTITY IN EXTRAORDINARY EXPERIENCES

The Concepts of Self and Identity

An individual sense of *self* and *identity* develops as a person interacts with others, learning and practicing the culture of a group. A simple definition of the self is that it is the "I" or "Me," an individual's reflective consciousness of being a separate human being (Mead 1934). *Identity* may be defined as "the ongoing sense the self has of who it is, as conditioned through its ongoing interactions with others. Identity is how the self conceives of itself and labels itself" (Mathews 2000:16–17). Identity is what people answer when they ask themselves the question, "Who am I?" Most people's answers are drawn from their cultural context. Typical answers include a mixture of cultural roles and relationships (e.g., mother, student, lawyer); personality qualities that are recognized in the culture (e.g., outgoing, agreeable, open);

and the purposes in life that give our lives meaning, which we have chosen from our culture (e.g., I have a passion for photography, or caring for my family).

Levels of the Cultural Self

Anthropologist Gordon Mathews has brilliantly analyzed the influence of culture on the self in his book *Global Culture/Individual Identity* (2000). According to Mathews, the "cultural shapings of self occur at what may analytically be viewed as three separate levels of consciousness"—"what you do without thinking, what you do because you have to, and what you do because you choose to" (Mathews 2000:12, 15–16).

The first and deepest level refers to the aspects of culture that are totally taken for granted, aspects that we are mostly not even conscious of. Such deep shaping includes the language that shapes our thinking, basic beliefs about reality, and the many aspects of our culture that are highly habitual (Mathews 2000:12–14). Mathews describes how as a teacher he brings his students' taken for granted beliefs to the surface—he tears up a $100 bill, and the students gasp, thus he shows them their taken-for-granted esteem for money (Mathews 2000:13). A good story about this deep level of the self was told in an article on collaboration in the journal *Parabola* (Svigals, et al. 2012):

> In an attempt to measure individual intelligence through a series of nonverbal puzzles, it has been rumored that anthropologists asked a group of aboriginal people to assemble a pile of interconnected blocks as quickly as possible. When the signal was given, they converged around the first pile and put it together in record time. Then they went down the line together, pile-by-pile. The anthropologists tried to explain that each person needed to work independently, but this rule was incomprehensive to people who saw themselves as inextricably connected to others in pursuing a communal purpose.

Another good example of the deep level of the cultural self is a psychological study by Taka Masuda. He asked students at Kyoto University and the University of Michigan to look at animated underwater scenes. The scenes depicted one or more "focal" fish, that were bigger and moving more quickly than anything else in the scenes, and also depicted less quickly moving animals, bubbles, plants, and inert items like rocks. After seeing the scenes, the students were asked to describe what they saw and their answers were coded as to whether they referred to the "focal" fish or the other objects. The students from American individualistic culture were much more likely to begin their statements with a reference to a "focal" fish, while the students from Japan's more collectively oriented culture were much more likely to begin with a reference to the setting, e.g., "it looked like a pond." The students from Kyoto University were 60 percent more likely to notice background elements, and 50 percent more likely to notice background elements that were inert (Nisbett 2003: 89–90).

A middle level of the cultural self includes behaviors we are conscious of, which Mathews refers to in Japanese as *shikata ga nai*, a term meaning "it can't be helped." This includes all the things we "do as members of our societies whether we like it or not," such as paying taxes, going to school or work, exhibiting behaviors appropriate to our gender, and obeying traffic regulations. As compared to the deeper level, this *shikata ga nai* is experienced as more outside the self, the social pressures on the self which the self "can't fully resist." We all shape our lives "within and against" such social pressures (Mathews 2000:14–15). Interestingly, researchers have found that when a person goes to live in a foreign culture, and begins to conform to externally induced behaviors, these may eventually be experienced as internally induced (Cross and Gore 2003:554).

The third, shallowest, level, is what Mathews calls the "the cultural supermarket." "This is the level at which selves sense that they freely pick and choose the ideas they want to live by." "In a given (affluent) society, one person may be devoted to Western classical music, another to Indian ragas, a third to grunge rock, and a fourth to reggae . . . one person may become a Christian, another a Buddhist, another an atheist, and a fourth a believer in a UFO cult." This choice of values and identities seems to be free, but it is not really totally free, in the sense that people are influenced by their genders, religious beliefs, and ethnicities, and in the sense that it happens within a "cultural supermarket that heavily advertises some choices and suppresses others" and also within social interaction with others requiring negotiations and performances (Mathews 2000:15). This level is shallow in comparison with the other levels, but paradoxically, it may be the level that seems most deeply meaningful to us, especially if we have never been made fully aware of the deeper levels.

Changes in the Self in Extraordinary Experiences

In my research I found that extraordinary experiences can lead people to change at any of the three levels of the cultural self-described by Mathews: the deepest, taken for granted, aspects of self and identity; the *shikata ga nai*, or "it can't be helped" practices dictated by culture; and the aspects of identity freely chosen from the "cultural supermarket."

More Superficial Levels

On the more superficial, but not unimportant, levels of the *shikata ga nai* and the "cultural supermarket," there can be a kind of enlargement of the self. Many people who go through extraordinary experiences describe themselves as growing and developing; they may attain an array of new personal skills and interests, or accomplish things that would have been impossible in their previous lives. Robert Parris Moses (Bob Moses), a founder of the Student Nonviolent Coordinating Committee, was later awarded a MacArthur Fellowship ("Genius Grant") for the community organizing skills he displayed during the Civil Rights Movement. He used these skills later in founding the successful Algebra Project, which enables disadvantaged minority children to master the math skills necessary to succeed in the current economy (Lewis 2009:288–94). Another civil rights worker, Theresa Del Pozzo, had developed administrative and organizing skills which she put to use after she left the Movement and worked representing reggae, pop, and jazz musicians. She could take on recording contract negotiations, due to her experience with legal matters; she could organize a band tour, given her experience organizing car caravans; she could function in developing countries like Jamaica, because she knew how to "make do" (Curry et al. 2000:200–203).

The two young soldiers I described above similarly portrayed themselves as having developed an array of useful skills. Smith, for example, described himself in high school as an introverted loner who was angry and miserable. He expressed gratitude that the military life had forced him to grow socially. He told me that he learned how to interact with people, developed an open mindedness to racial and ethnic diversity, and explored new kinds of music and dance. Many soldiers also pride themselves on the combat skills they learn. For example, *Seal Team Six,* a memoir of Howard E. Wasdin's service with the Navy Seals, can be read as a kind of extended reflection on the extraordinary prowess a member of this elite unit must attain (Wasdin and Templin 2011). Beaumont, the young Marine I interviewed, talked about how the Marines train soldiers to be killers and inspire them with the confidence they can kill and the desire to do so. He described his "excitement" in Afghanistan when his unit was sent to ambush a large number of the enemy, excitement that he would finally be doing what he had been trained to do in service to his country. Joe Gardner, another American veteran I interviewed, spoke with pride about how his service as a supply sergeant in the National Guard in Afghanistan had taught him logistical skills, critical thinking, and in general showed him "what I have to do to be a professional." Another former soldier, Vietnam veteran, Philip Caputo, acknowledged his military skills but viewed them in a more ironic light. In his memoir, *A Rumor of War*, he said:

> At the age of twenty-four, I was more prepared for death than I was for life . . . I was almost completely ignorant about the stuff of ordinary life, about marriage, mortgages, and building a career. I had a degree, but no skills. I had never run an office, taught a class, built a bridge, welded, programmed a computer, laid bricks, sold anything, or operated a lathe. But I had acquired some expertise in the art of killing. I knew how to face death and how to cause

it, with everything on the evolutionary scale of weapons from the knife to the
3.5 inch rocket launcher (1977:3).

During the civil war in El Salvador in the 1970s and 1980s, many peasant
women joined the revolutionary Farabundo Marti National Liberation Front
(FMLN) and participated in combat as guerrillas or in military support work.
Others stayed in their villages but were active as collaborators. Prior to the
revolution, the women had played traditional roles as spouses and mothers.
As activists, they learned new skills, as combatants, medics, and radio opera-
tors. Some who had spent time in refugee camps before joining the FMLN
had received an elementary education and worked as teachers in the revolution. Ironically, according to researcher Jocelyn Viterna, the women who
were combat guerrillas, the most "gender-bending" option, were the least
likely to be active later in their communities after demobilization and the
most likely to lead private, domestically-oriented lives. This is because, in an
echo of Caputo, their skills did not translate as well into peacetime work as
did skills such as literacy and medicine (Viterna 2013: 183–95, 199–202).

In extraordinary experiences there are many *shikata ga nai* rituals of daily
life. We saw examples of this in chapter 1, from the daily roll call at Auschwitz to marches at boot camp. Interestingly, examples of a kind of happiness
or satisfaction are often found in these "it can't be helped" routines. Caputo's
book on his Vietnam experience is an example. After describing the brutality
and fear of his months in basic training, he wrote of the happiness he felt at
nearing the end of a day of endless marching under a remorseless sun.

> Now that it knew it was on the last leg, the company began to march faster,
> almost jauntily. A few marines near the point started singing the verse to a
> marching song and the rest of the column answered with the chorus . . . The
> song was like a cry of defiance. They had just humped through thirty miles of
> wilderness in intense heat with forty pounds on their backs, and they were
> coming in singing. Nothing could subdue them. Hearing that full throated
> *Whoa-oh-oh-oh Little Liza, Little Liza Jane* roaring through the woods, I felt
> proud of that spirited company and happy that I was one of them (Caputo
> 1977:19–20).

Viktor Frankl, the well-known psychiatrist who survived Auschwitz, described this sort of happiness as "negative happiness." He wrote, "We were
grateful for the smallest of mercies. We were glad when there was time to
delouse before going to bed, although in itself this was no pleasure, as it
meant standing naked in an unheated hut where icicles hung from the ceiling.
But we were thankful if there was no air raid during this operation and the
lights were not switched off. If we could not do the job properly, we were
kept awake half the night" (Frankl 1963:74).

I interviewed Linda Nelson, a former Catholic nun. The convent she entered had a daily routine that included waking up at 5:00 AM to the sound of a bell; being in the chapel for prayer and meditation at 5:30; keeping silence from the time of the evening bell until breakfast was over; doing chores silently; going to classes and taking part in a recreation period. Every nine days there was a gathering in which participants were expected to describe their sins. Nelson especially enjoyed the peacefulness of the silence; it was "meditative," "a good place to be." She also enjoyed the sense of belonging with others, the classes, and the recreational activities.

Deepest Level

Extraordinary experiences also lead to transformations at the deepest levels of the cultural self. I interviewed Anita Schorr, a child survivor of the Holocaust, who spoke of the negative changes to self and identity she suffered as a result of her experiences. She was a young Jewish Czechoslovakian girl of nine when the Germans invaded the country. She had grown up in a loving middle class family; her father was a salesman in the textile industry, and an officer in the Czechoslovakian military, whose real love was music and sports. Schorr loved opera and other music, and she became confident of her strength and skills through taking part in various sports. After the invasion, the Nazis rounded up the Jews and Schorr's family was taken to Auschwitz where she remained until the age of fourteen. When they arrived at Auschwitz, her father was separated from the family and sent elsewhere to be a laborer. When the guards began a process of separating the women who were healthy and old enough to work from those deemed not so, her mother pushed her away and told her to go with the adult women—"tell them you are eighteen!" her mother said. Schorr complied, but with a heavy heart. She believed for years after, that her mother had sent her away because she didn't love her, not understanding that her mother was trying to save her life. In this way, her understanding of herself in relation to her parents was profoundly altered. She went from a person who might have said "I am beloved," to one who might have said, "I am unloved." Schorr also harbored resentment against her father for not getting the family out of the country when this might have been possible, for not fighting and instead just going quietly when ordered to go. He had believed that his being an officer in the military would protect them, and was "an optimist bordering on stupid." From Auschwitz, Schorr was sent to Hamburg, Germany, with thousands of adult women, where she labored nearly a year on dreadful assignments, such as going through the rubble in bombed buildings to drag out the corpses. After that, she was sent to Bergen-Belsen, where she remained until liberation at the end of the war. Resilient, Schorr survived by what she described as "making myself invisible," and also "hope and perseverance." She does not believe, as many Holocaust survivors do, that she survived simply due to good luck. She survived partly by pluck. The self-confidence nurtured in her by her family was not erased by the Nazis. Once, she and the other women were stealing apples on the way to and from a camp to work. Other women who got caught were beaten. When Schorr was caught, she spoke out, "I have apples because we are hungry!" The apples were taken away but she was not beaten. However, despite her resilience, after the war ended, she felt "mutilated," especially because she had lost her opportunity for education. She overate, and weighed over 200 pounds by the time she was in her early twenties. She tried to put the past behind her, saying "I put my little armor on," but she suffered from nightmares for around twenty years. Schorr emigrated first to Israel, then, in 1959, to the United States, and for many years never told her story. She was plagued with questions like, "Why didn't more Jews fight back?" and "Why did I survive?" I will discuss Schorr's transition further in chapter 4.

Meaning in the Cultural Supermarket

Some choices in the cultural supermarket of extraordinary experiences become an intensely felt part of the self. As mentioned above, although chosen experiences may be more superficial than those at the deeper and more unconscious level of the self, this does not mean that they are not highly meaningful to individuals and important in their lives. Extraordinary experiences lead some people to develop new purposes in life and to choose to see the meaning of their lives in a completely new way. Nando Parrado, whose story was presented in chapter 1, began to see his purpose in life completely differently. Before the disastrous plane crash in the Andes, he had been a relatively carefree young man, living in the moment, without thinking more deeply about the meaning of life. During his confrontation with death in the mountains, he became more and more aware of an enormous love for his father. He was filled with joy at his memory of his father, who was at home missing him. He suddenly realized that

> Death has an opposite, but the opposite is not mere living. It is not courage or faith or human will. The opposite of death is *love*. How had I missed that? How does anyone miss that? Love is our only weapon. Only love can turn mere life into a miracle, and draw precious meaning from suffering and fear. For a brief, magical moment, all my fears lifted, and I knew that I would not let death control me. I would walk through the godforsaken country that separated me from my home with love and hope in my heart (Parrado 2006:201).

Viktor Frankl, the psychiatrist, examined the meaning of suffering in his experiences in Auschwitz. He pointed out that even in the worst of imposed conditions, humans have the "spiritual freedom" to choose to find meaning in their suffering. A few prisoners endured the horrors of Auschwitz "rising above outward fate" with bravery, dignity, or unselfishness. They attained values through their suffering that made the suffering meaningful (Frankl 1963:116–17). Frankl advised fellow prisoners to think of future goals, to have faith they would survive to achieve them. He envisioned a time in his own future when he was giving a lecture, in a warm room, to an attentive audience, on the psychology of the concentration camps. Responsibility toward a loved one waiting for the prisoner to return, the goal of finishing an unfinished book, such meaningful purposes to one's life made suffering meaningful (Frankl 1963:118–25).

Child soldiers are often pursuing purposes that are deeply meaningful to them. We miss this if we see them simply as victims manipulated by adults and caught up in conflicts they had no part in. Mike Wessels has written about "*unforced recruitment*" of child soldiers.

> In apartheid South Africa, black township youth—the Young Lions—adopted an ideology of liberation, which gave meaning to the harsh realities of their existence and conferred a clear sense of identity and direction. In Guatemala, many children of landless peasants living in extreme poverty and victimized by repressive regimes embraced an ideology of revolution . . . In Rwanda during the early 1990s, the Hutu-dominated government used radio to spread hatred of the Tutsis who were demonized as murderous outsiders. This helped prepare children for roles as killers in the youth militias in the 1994 genocide (Wessells 1997:32–39).

We saw in chapter 1 that Ishmael Beah came to closely embrace the goal of killing people he saw as having murdered his own family.

The Self as a Construction The Concepts of Agency and Engulfment in the Self and Identity

Even though our self and identity are shaped by culture, we are also active agents who are making choices about how the process unfolds. The concept of *agency* highlights the active part played by the individual in constructing the self. Human agency occurs in part because each of us has basic biological and psychological needs we must try to meet. These needs include the need for physical subsistence and security, the need for connection with others, the need to have a meaning or purpose to life, and the need to have a sense of self and personal autonomy (Rosenberg 2003). Individuals are constantly strategizing how to meet basic needs in ways that are drawn from the culture in which they are situated. Most people choose strategies that are appropriate, or at least tolerated, in the culture. Thus to fulfill the need for connection, one person may choose to join a social movement, another to marry; to fulfill the need for meaning, one person may choose to join the military, another to practice a sport. Some people of course become rebels or revolutionaries who strategize to meet their needs in ways that are not culturally appropriate and over time this process may even result in cultural change. But even rebels and revolutionaries are not necessarily original; they may be drawing upon a "counter culture" of disobedience with a rich history.

The Self as a Construction

As a result of agency, the self and identity are perpetually under construction. Social science research has revealed that as we strive to meet our needs, we are continually working on our sense of self, our identities, even our psychological and biological functioning, constructing and reconstructing ourselves. Here are some ways we do this:

First, like actors on a stage, we *present* ourselves to others so that they will view us the way we would like to be viewed. This idea was first elaborated by sociologist Erving Goffman, who termed it "presentation of self" (Goffman 1959, 1963). In Goffman's "dramaturgical" analysis, the self is in this sense a *performance.* For example, a waitress who finds her purpose in life through going to college to become a professional, may bring this up in conversations with the customers in an effort to ensure that they see her the way she sees herself. We saw earlier how Anita Schorr presented herself as a plucky young woman and that this enabled her to avoid punishment for stealing apples. Even aspects of identity that may seem "innate" to us require activity on our part to make them happen—after years of socialization, we may do it unconsciously, but we are still *doing* something. For example, we construct or present our genders by choice of dress, haircut, makeup, and behaviors of all sorts (Butler 2006).

Presentation of self includes *emotions management,* working to contain those feelings that are culturally inappropriate and convey those that are appropriate (Hochschild 2003). Corporations in today's world have heightened the practice of emotions management by requiring that employees display emotions considered best suited to corporate goals. For example, the checkout clerk at the store may smile as he gives us our change and say, "Have a great day!" regardless of whether he really feels happy or friendly. We saw in chapter 1 how Ron Kovic struggled to keep his fearful emotions under control while in boot camp. Prathia Hall, a participant in the Civil Rights Movement, has noted that civil rights workers endeavored to use their fear as part of a "survival kit." "The challenge was to use fear as a signal to exercise caution while refusing to allow fear to paralyze you" (Hall 2012:178).

Second, we engage in *narrative practices,* that is, we tell ourselves stories, often quite elaborate, about ourselves, and present stories about ourselves to others (Holstein and Gubrium 2000; McAdams 1997, 2008, 2013). For example, when we go out on a date with a new person, we might tell our date about our life history with a focus on how we developed our current purposes in life. We saw in chapter 1 that Primo Levi, while in the concentration camp, was engaged in constructing a narrative about his experiences there, to expose the Nazi cruelties to the world once he was free again. In storytelling, we integrate life experiences into an evolving story of the self, which helps us meet our need for meaning or purpose.

Third, we may rank our multiple identities in an order of importance. The concept of *identity salience* refers to the point that we may find one or more of our identities more important or meaningful than others, and actively engage with it more than with others (Stryker 1980, Stets and Burke 2003: 134–35, Ritzer 2005, entry under "identity," Viterna 2013). For example, a parent may see the identity of parent as more meaningful than the identities of worker or student, and when choices must be made, endeavor to prioritize the activities of parent. We saw earlier the salience for Nando Parrado of his identity as his father's son.

This process of construction and reconstruction of self can be quite difficult, especially in today's complex multicultural societies. The self is not as simple or unitary as it might be in a simpler culture, and we may experience ourselves as one self in one setting, and another in another. The self can become "saturated" with multiple possibilities. This can be burdensome if a person is struggling to juggle competing identities, but it can also be liberating if a person is opening up to new possibilities (Gergen 1991).

Limitations of Agency: Engulfment

As we interact with our culture to construct our sense of self and identity, sometimes culture "gets the upper hand" so to speak and human agency is diminished. This phenomenon has been described under a variety of terms by sociologists who have studied how individuals can be constrained by the social statuses they occupy and the roles they play. One concept is *role engulfment,* meaning a situation in which a person becomes profoundly wrapped up in a particular cultural role (Schur 1971). Sociologists have studied role engulfment in populations such as the homeless and college basketball players (Snow and Anderson 1993; Adler and Adler 1991). Role engulfment contrasts with *role distance,* in which people feel a greater inner separation from a role they are playing (Ritzer 2005: 651–55; Goffman 1961). Another sociological idea is that of *master status,* a position one holds that has a major effect on a person's life, superseding other statuses in a person's eyes and in the eyes of others. Stigmatized statuses (i.e., those that are looked down upon by others), often become master statuses (Hughes 1945; Allport 1954).

I believe it is helpful to extend the concept of role engulfment to speak also of *cultural engulfment,* which I define as a situation in which a person's self and identity are highly bound up with *various* aspects of the culture of a group (i.e., beyond the particular role they are playing). This can include the purpose and meaning of life as defined in the culture, political ideology, interpretations of history, norms about family and friendship, etc. Cultural engulfment implies that a person can become so wrapped up in the new culture's worldview that the person's previous worldview is superseded, or the person is unable to see that there are choices *not* contained within that new worldview.

Some people acquire a completely new identity derived from participation in an extraordinary community. In this identity, some also experience role engulfment and/or cultural engulfment. I suspect that engulfment occurs in part because of the great political, moral, historical or spiritual significance that people attach to their experiences. For example, many who participated in the Civil Rights Movement felt their identities came to be completely associated with the ideal and reality of working and living in an integrated community, striving for the "Beloved Community" of Martin Luther King, Jr. Penny Patch wrote about how she even began to lose her sense of whiteness:

> My awareness of myself as one of very few white people in a crowd of black people rapidly diminished. Did I notice in the beginning? Probably so. But within a few weeks conscious awareness faded, and the sensation for me was of melting into the crowd. If I looked at my arm, I could see I was white, but if I looked at other people, which is more often what I was doing, then I would see people just like me. Or rather, what happened is that I came to feel I looked just like them (Curry et al. 2000:143).

Patch recognized that this was an illusion, and one that could be dangerous in the context of the Jim Crow South. Another white civil rights worker, Theresa del Pozzo, wrote that her experience

> was the beginning of seeing the world through black eyes . . . the movement was happening within the African-American community, and so whites who came to work in the movement lived within that world. It was a real eye opener for me when . . . as a white, I became part of a small minority. In the movement, black folks were at home; this was their world, they could speak and act naturally. They weren't on guard, as in the white world . . . Being there and seeing the world from their perspective had a profound impact on me and forever altered the way I would perceive the patterns of American racism (Curry et al. 2000:187,191).

I interviewed Mark Alessi, a long time aid worker in developing nations in African and Southeast Asia. Alessi has worked in many post conflict situations, primarily as a country director with European NGOs; he has helped local people rebuild housing and markets, reconcile peacefully with former enemies, reintegrate child soldiers and street children, and develop economic and educational infrastructures. He experienced the horrors of civil war in Burundi and Liberia, and its aftermath in Sierra Leone and Uganda. He described himself as an "ex-pat" (expatriate), an American who works in foreign countries. Alessi is highly engaged with the ex-pat culture and his work roles. He said, "what *I* do, where *I* live, is a normal life," not the life Americans live in America. Alessi described himself as a world citizen, someone who prefers to live in developing countries, and prides himself on his stance of helping people help themselves rather than imposing American values and procedures. Alessi said he is happy with his life where "my work is service," even though often hard and dangerous. He is "grateful" and "humbled" that local people welcome him in and allow him to assist them as they work to develop a better life for their children. To Alessi, many people in countries like Burundi and Uganda seem happy, but not many Americans seem happy and their lives seem "shallow" and "superficial" by contrast.

Michel Girodo, a professor at the University of Ottowa, interviewed undercover agents working for drug and law enforcement agencies. Some operatives were undercover for lengthy assignments of six to eight months, and some underwent a "wholesale transformation of identity," by which he meant they received a new name, life history, fake documents, clothing, places to live, etc. The fake role and the settings they were placed in (e.g., drug communities, motorcycle gangs, etc.) became their only social reality, since their only contact with the world they had left would be through a "coverman." Isolated, and very lonely, it was not unusual for agents to be "won over" to their fake role and new associates. Girodo gave the example of an agent who became reluctant to testify against people he had become friendly with, and on a day he was supposed to buy drugs from them, hid the drugs in order to be able to say that he had been unsuccessful (Girodo 1984:172–74).

Robert Killian was an undercover agent for the Orange County Sheriff's Office in central Florida from 2003 to 2010. He infiltrated the Outlaws motorcycle gang and the first SS Kavallerie Brigade, the motorcycle division of the neo-Nazi Aryan Nations organization. Killian presented himself as a neo-Nazi biker named "Doc." He wore a biker vest and Nazi jewelry. He learned how to laugh at racist jokes and to sit in when others discussed crimes the groups had committed or when they planned new crimes. Killian told interviewers Heidi Beirich and Laurie Wood, "I didn't feel like I changed my personality for the role; (but) maybe the role was starting to change my personality a little bit." His family began to notice the changes. "I became more secretive, less trustful of everybody, including my chain of command and co-workers. Those relationships (were) getting distant in slow increments." Killian began to develop empathy for the extremists he was spending so much of his life with. "You start to know these bad guys at a level you don't normally see them. You're starting to see how they interact with their children. They're treating you like a very close friend and even sometimes like a family member. But this is a bad guy I'm eventually going to have to put in jail." Killian had not been prepared for the wrenching changes to his life. His marriage began to fall apart, and ended in divorce. Today he is always on alert, aware that there could be reprisals from the people he helped bring to justice. Charlie Fuller, Executive Director of the International Association of Undercover Officers told the *Intelligence Report* that most officers who go undercover are not prepared for the stress involved from living two lives and from having to betray friends. "It eats at you while you're doing it, and it eats at you after you do it. It haunts you. You think . . . it will never go away as long as I live." Fuller also said, "When (the operation) is over, you're asking 'What do I do now? Where is my identity?' Then you have to go back to shuffling papers at your desk. You can't just turn that off" (Beirich and Wood, 2012:17–20).

I interviewed a State Police officer, John Lerner, who had been an undercover agent at one point during his career. He had never been under deep cover, was always returning to his home and family after work, and described himself as having a strong sense of who he was apart from the roles he played. Even so, Lerner did sometimes feel empathy for the people he was getting information from and struggled to handle it. He would tell himself that the best thing he could do for them was to help shut down the drug operation that was ruining their lives. He described one of the highlights of his experience as helping one of his informants get into a rehab place and out of the drug life.

One aspect of cultural engulfment and role engulfment is that *shared* identity becomes highly significant. People who have been immersed in extraordinary experiences such as military combat, revolution and social movements, even prison, often come to see their fellows as buddies or comrades, and this shared identity takes on a compelling importance. Catherine Lynn Brooks interviewed "lifers" in prison in Canada for her Master's Thesis at the University of Windsor. She learned that being a lifer in prison has a high status; lifers are respected and expected to stand out from the ordinary prisoner. As a result, lifers have more in common with one another than they do with other prisoners or with people of their own age in the outside world. Sometimes lifers are released, and even then, continue to identify more with having been a lifer than with new statuses in the ordinary world (Brooks 2003:42 ff;73,86). Accounts of military service contain many references to the idea that soldiers fight for their buddies as much as they fight against the enemy. The young veterans I interviewed certainly expressed this point of view. A young Vietnam veteran interviewed by Murray Polner characterized his relationships with other soldiers as a "brotherhood of blood," even though the war was not something he wanted to die for, and he returned from

Vietnam a "Dove" (Polner 1971: 67). Interesting examples of comradeship can be found in the interviews with South African revolutionaries of the African National Congress, which have been collected in the ANC Oral History Project archived at the University of Connecticut. Many were in prison for a number of years, enduring conditions such as torture, daily strip searches, breaking rocks under the hot sun, and terrible food; visitors were rare, often it would be years between visits. The ANC prisoners stuck together, fought the authorities, and managed to communicate with the outside world, with the result that over time, conditions improved somewhat. Nikosinathi B. Fihla, who was imprisoned for thirteen years, stated that he had told his family that "we are married to you but also to the organization" (Fihla 2005:32). Denis Goldberg, who was also in prison for many years, characterized the ANC community within the prison as being full of love, trust, togetherness, affection, comradeship, and intense support (Goldberg 2005:29). A number of those interviewed expressed that they later missed the camaraderie of their prison years.

In the previous pages, I have explored the ways in which the culture of extraordinary experiences affects the individual, especially through the phenomenon of culture shock, and the reshaping of self and identity, including engulfment. Individuals can also be *biologically* altered by extraordinary experiences. The mind and body can undergo changes, which in turn, can have an impact on the person's sense of self and identity. In the following sections, I explore the concepts of *habit* and *trauma*.

THE CONCEPT OF CULTURE AND HABIT

Culture affects individuals even on a biological level, by affecting the functioning of the brain and other bodily systems. We have already gotten a glimpse of how culture can affect people on a biological level, in examining the state of culture shock. Scientific research shows that depression involves changes in brain chemistry and structure. Thus when a person experiences depression during the second stage of culture shock, the stress of exposure to a different culture may be literally changing the brain in a way that is not entirely under conscious control. Culture also affects us on a biological level in the phenomenon of *habit*. As mentioned above, habits are routine patterns of thoughts, emotions, and behaviors. In the phenomenon of habit, all manner of culturally appropriate thoughts, feelings, and actions are performed by our minds and bodies in a highly routine, even unconscious way (Camic 1986; Bourdieu 1990).

Examples of Culture and Habit in Extraordinary Experiences

Extraordinary experiences can lead people to develop new habits of behavior that are not easily shed. In my view, these can exist at any of the three levels of the cultural self. Beaumont, the young Marine, sleeps with a knife under his bed. If he hears a noise in the night, he gets up, pulls the knife out, and patrols the house to make sure everything is all right. Linda Nelson, the former Catholic nun I interviewed, told me that she had become so accustomed to the habit of silence in the convent that when she left and returned to her family, she once threw a teacup at her mother when her mother was yelling at her stepfather about his drinking, and was about to hit him. Joe Gardner, the young National Guard veteran I interviewed, told me he is only able to sleep about four hours a night. When in combat in Afghanistan he got used to "sleeping with my eyes open," and "staying up three or four days."

Habits of behavior at the deepest level can be complex. I interviewed Eva Lukacs, another child survivor of the Holocaust in an Eastern European country. Her Jewish parents had tried to save her life by placing her with Christians. Her first placement was with a poor Christian woman who taught her how to say Christian prayers. Eva went from an affluent middle class life to living in a shack with a packed dirt floor, no running water, and only an outhouse. This home was soon destroyed in the war, and she was placed in another home that was also eventually destroyed. The city was under siege, and Lukacs ended up one of a group of 100 children who lived on the streets and in bombed out houses, under the care of a few adults, freezing and starving, and then in a home of some sort where the children got lice and became ill. Lukacs told me that as a result of all this, "I don't want to lose control." She developed a deep need to control her life, which she felt was in reaction to the almost complete absence of control during the time she was separated from her family. Sometimes, she said, habits she developed in order to keep herself in control have been a big disadvantage; for example, when she couldn't sleep, she would like to have taken a sleeping pill, and didn't, because she felt that she just didn't want to "let go." Her deep seated habits of mind affected her for years. She also felt like an outsider, "a nobody." Lukacs said that she once saw a psychiatrist who told her that now, "you are no longer a pariah." But Lukacs said "in the back of my mind, I was." She stated that in the United States, it can be detrimental to your career if you don't "puff yourself up." But Holocaust survivors always struggle with a feeling, "you were nobody, so don't pretend to be somebody."

Trauma

The interaction between biology and culture also comes into play in the realm of *trauma* because of how the brain records traumatic experiences in memory and reacts to those memories. A traumatic event has been classically defined by Judith Herman as one in which "the victim is rendered helpless by overwhelming force" (Herman 1992:33). The realm of trauma more closely fits the public perception that people who go through extraordinary experiences are changed by *dramatic events.* But culture comes into play even here, since the overwhelming force that renders the victim helpless is often ultimately cultural in origin. For example, a civil war may result from economic collapse connected to downturns in the world market, and its combatants may experience the events of the war within particular military cultures (e.g., the culture of an official army or the culture of a paramilitary group). Even the events of "natural" disasters are often connected to culture. For example, organizational and institutional failures may result in the collapse of an unsafe mine or levees that are breached by waves during a hurricane, and survivors go through the events of the disaster and its aftermath within particular cultures.

Memories of traumatic experiences become deeply imprinted in the brain. When a person leaves a traumatic experience, it is not easily shaken off. Those suffering from "Post Traumatic Stress Disorder" (PTSD) have problems such as nightmares, flashbacks, and hypersensitivity (e.g. to loud noises). Even when such overt symptoms are not present, a person may be perpetually on guard, the brain anxiously working to protect the self from dangers that could reoccur. Thus memory and emotions function to ensure that the traumatized person's sense of self and identity is not ephemeral or delicate, but a strong, bodily-based entity that has a new life of its own (Herman 1992; Salzer 2011:xii–xxv).

I want to remind the reader that not all extraordinary experiences are traumatic. For example, not all social movement participants are placed in situations in which they are "rendered helpless." Nor do all individuals who are exposed to traumatic events suffer afterward from PTSD or other psychological problems. However, enough extraordinary experiences *do* involve stressful, traumatic events, and enough returnees *do* suffer, so it is important to look at trauma in some depth. Herman has pointed out that "traumatic events overwhelm the ordinary systems of care that give people a sense of control, connection, and meaning . . . (and) overwhelm the ordinary human adaptations to life" (Herman 1992:33–34). Trauma changes our sense of self and identity in ways we may not even be conscious of because they are at such a deep and highly habitual level. Memories of the frightening event are wired into our brain in a way that keeps them immediate, with all the original sights, sounds, and emotions just like they were when we had the experience. This contrasts with memories of normal events, which are processed by the brain in such a way that our brains know they are in the past. We remember things about normal events that are meaningful to us, but the immediacy and emotional saliency are gone. Traumatic events probably do not get processed this way, because the events so strongly activate our sympathetic nervous system (the locus of the "fight or flight" response) that the brain systems cannot go back to functioning properly. There are several consequences: the traumatized mind is always on high alert, scanning the environment for danger. Second, memories of the traumatic events often intrude into the present moment, or haunt one's sleep as nightmares. Finally, the mind may play tricks on itself in an effort at relief, creating feelings of detachment from oneself, or a kind of numbness (Herman 1992:35–45).

Because of such symptoms, people living with trauma are literally no longer themselves, whether they fully realize it or not. In general, traumatized people develop self-protective habits. They may avoid people and activities that they fear might expose them to re-experiencing the traumatic events, inadvertently considerably narrowing their relationships, and constricting their meaningful activities and purposes in life. They may also constrict their relationships, activities, and purposes because they lack trust in others, lack self-confidence, or feel shame or guilt. Positive emotions which were once characteristic of their identity, or could be, such as confidence, openness, trust, or feeling empowered, are truncated (Herman 1992:33–45). Psychiatrist Alicia Salzer has termed this condition "permatrauma," and described it as a state of continually re-traumatizing oneself by being perpetually self-protective (Salzer, 2011:xii–xxv).

Many of the traumas resulting from extraordinary experiences seem to fall into the category of what Herman calls "*complex* post-traumatic stress disorder." She pointed out that there is a difference between traumatic events that are one-time, such as a single combat incident, a rape, or an accident, and those that occur over a period of months to years, such as survivors of prolonged captivity, some religious cults, domestic violence, or childhood sexual abuse. While any traumatic experience can have lasting effects, as discussed above—hyperarousal, intrusion, constriction—the effects of an experience of long duration are more intense and complicated. Interestingly, Herman comments: "Because post-traumatic symptoms are so persistent and so wide-ranging, they may be mistaken for enduring characteristics of the victim's personality. This is a costly error." She included an insightful quote from a portrait Doris Lessing wrote of her father, a World War I combat veteran: "The young bank clerk who worked such long hours for so little money, but who danced, sang, played, flirted—this naturally vigorous, sensuous being was killed in 1914, 1915, 1916 . . . The people I've met . . . who knew him young speak of his high spirits, his energy, his enjoyment of life . . . I do not think these people would have easily recognized the ill, irritable, abstracted, hypochondriac man I knew" (Herman 1992:49).

CULTURE, SELF, AND IDENTITY IN EXITING THE
EXTRAORDINARY: AN IRONY

In this chapter I have argued that extraordinary experiences are often felt as drastic and deep changes in self and identity. When we leave our familiar cultures for extraordinary experiences, we are not bystanders. Our routine and habitual behaviors are undermined. The compromises we made with one social world disappear and we are forced to make new ones. Our freedom to choose may seem to be shrinking. The person we thought we were has suddenly vanished, and we are not quite sure whom this new person is who has shown up. This can be an exhilarating experience—and often is, when the extraordinary experience was *chosen*, as in the case of the new member of the religious cult, the volunteer soldier, the undercover agent, or the revolutionary "true believer" (Hoffer 2002). Or it can be a degrading one—and often is, when the extraordinary experience was *not* chosen, as in the case of the prisoner, the concentration camp inmate, the draftee or the disaster victim. As time passes, people construct a new self and a new identity. If we are in the extraordinary world long enough, we are likely to end up with an identity that is greatly changed. We may develop a new, taken-for-granted layer of the self, based on the extraordinary world's culture. We may internalize those aspects of culture to the point that we are no longer conscious of them as outside ourselves. We may also become habituated to new practices of *shikata ga nai* that work for us in the extraordinary culture. And we make new free choices from those available to us in the extraordinary culture's "supermarket." Often, in extraordinary cultures, culture gets the upper hand, and we abandon our past and become engulfed by a new identity or even a whole new worldview. Some people may exist with a greater state of tension between the old and the new; they may maintain more distance from the new self and identity, or find a way to carry old identities over into the new world. But either way, the self and identity are tangibly transformed by the extraordinary experience. We come to present ourselves differently. We feel and show our emotions differently. We tell different stories about ourselves and others. We are someone else, not the person we used to be. If and when we return to the ordinary world, we no longer move in it in the easy way we once did. As one of the child survivors of the Holocaust said to me, "none of us are *ever* 'normal.'"

There is a certain irony in all of this. Although extraordinary experiences seem so unusual from the perspective of the ordinary world, it is exactly the same sort of cultural processes that shaped us to be the person we were in the ordinary world, that shape us to be the person we become in the extraordinary world. The two worlds are in this sense mirrors of one another. This fact is not only ironic—it is also ultimately liberating because as social scientists have pointed out, if all reality is humanly constructed, then another world is possible, and we are free to reconstruct our cultures and ourselves in ways that meet human needs better than the current ones do.

UNANSWERED QUESTIONS

As mentioned in the Introduction, since this book is an exploratory study, I have not answered every possible question about the topic. However, I can point out to the reader, at relevant points in the book, certain unanswered questions that are worthy of further study. One question I have not delved into in this chapter is the question of important differences among extraordinary experiences. It is possible that these differences influence the transformation of self and identity in extraordinary experiences, but I did not learn enough about this from my sources to warrant making generalizations about the matter.

We have already seen some of these differences. First, the dimension of choice. As noted above, some experiences are voluntary (being a war correspondent), others involuntary (being a prisoner). Some involuntary experiences, such as torture, reduce human agency to near zero. Second, the dimension of duration. Some are shorter (plane crash in Chile), others longer, years, a large chunk of a lifetime (revolutionaries in prison in South Africa). Third, the dimension of the nature of the events involved, and their impact on mind and body. Some are more likely to be traumatic (concentration camp), others are less likely to be traumatic (State Police undercover agent). Fourth, the dimension of isolation from the ordinary world. Some experiences entail a high degree of isolation from the ordinary world (child soldiers), others a lesser degree (war correspondents). Fifth, there is the dimension of formality. In some experiences, participants are socialized into the extraordinary culture in a planned, formal way, (Auschwitz), while in others, the culture is developed more spontaneously (plane crash in Chile). Finally, the dimension of isolation from fellow participants. Some experiences entail more isolation (torture victims may be held and tortured alone, although their captivity takes place within the organizational culture of a particular prison or military unit), others less isolation (civil rights workers). One might speculate that an experience that is long in duration, voluntary, and formal (e.g., being a volunteer soldier) might be more likely to result in engulfment, as compared with one that is shorter, involuntary, and informal. Perhaps a reader will decide to carry the investigation further in this direction.

Another question I have not covered in this chapter is the prevalence of PTSD after extraordinary experiences that are traumatic. Resilient individuals may go through traumatic events without many negative symptoms or may recover from symptoms over time. It is not clear whether such individuals are in the majority or minority. One estimate based on research into children who had an adverse early childhood is that only one in ten people are exceptionally resilient (Herman 1992:58–59). But a researcher who studies the United States military has reported that 85 percent of combat veterans are highly resilient and have no lasting symptoms from their experiences (Rendon 2012). The U.S. Department of Veterans Affairs has estimated that PTSD affects almost 31 percent of Vietnam War veterans, 10 percent of Persian Gulf veterans, 11 percent of veterans of the war in Afghanistan, and 20 percent of Iraq war veterans (Badger 2014). One difficulty in arriving at accurate statistics is that PTSD may show up many years after a traumatic experience. For example, some World War II veterans and Holocaust survivors have developed PTSD only when they were very elderly (Aarts and Op Den Velde 1996). Determination of statistics for the U.S. military may be complicated by a growing cultural expectation that soldiers will have PTSD when they return from deployment. Sociologist Jerry Lembcke has made a persuasive argument in *PTSD: Diagnosis and Identity in Post-empire America* (2013) that PTSD has increasingly become socially constructed as an expected state for returnees by film, television, journalism, psychiatry, and psychotherapy. If this is the case, I would expect that returnees may self-diagnose and medical practitioners may over diagnose, with an unknown influence on the statistics. Lembcke makes the argument not to deny the reality of PTSD, or to deprive veterans of needed care, but to caution us against facile assumptions about the prevalence of PTSD that portray veterans only as victims and mask a wider range of responses to war experiences, including political opposition to war (Lembcke 2014). Perhaps other researchers will pin down the answer to the question of the prevalence of PTSD among people returning from extraordinary experiences. It is an important question that was beyond the scope of the research for this book.

This chapter has discussed some typical aspects of the transformation of self and identity within the culture of extraordinary experiences, using concepts from the social sciences as a framework. This chapter concludes part I of the book, which has investigated the two questions: *What are extraordinary experiences? Why are people so profoundly altered by going through extraordinary experiences?* Now that I have explored some answers to these questions in part I, in part II I will proceed to examine the process of returning to the ordinary world.

Part II

Returning to the Ordinary World

Chapter Three

Contexts of Return

Part I explored two questions: *What are extraordinary experiences?* and *Why are people so profoundly altered by going through such experiences?* Chapter 1 portrayed seven cases of extraordinary experiences as they were remembered by participants. Chapter 2, drawing on the social sciences, made the analytical point that extraordinary experiences are an immersion in an extraordinary *cultural* world, one that shapes the self and identity, and the mind and body, just as all cultures do. With this background, I now turn, in part II, to the five central questions of the remainder of the book: *What social contexts do people return to after extraordinary experiences? What challenges do returnees face? What strategies have returnees used to face those challenges? Can any of these strategies help a returnee become happy or satisfied in the ordinary world? How can other people support returnees?*

This chapter explores the contexts faced by returnees when they go back to the ordinary world. Something that leaped out at me when I began investigating the return process is that there is no uniform "homecoming." The challenges faced by individual returnees, and how effectively they can deal with them, are greatly influenced by the diverse social conditions that confront them upon their return. In this chapter, I will sketch out several dimensions of the social context. First, on a societal level, what is the general attitude towards the returnees? Is it positive? or negative? or a mixed picture? Second, on the more intimate levels of family and community, have these groups been affected in some way by the extraordinary situation? And what are the attitudes of family members toward the returnees? Finally, are the problems of returnees recognized institutionally in any way? Are there any public policies or programs to facilitate re-entry, either on the national or local levels? After considering these topics in this chapter, in chapter 4, I explore the primary challenges people face when they return to the ordinary world. In chapter 5 I explore some strategies returnees have typically followed, as individuals, to deal with their challenges. In chapter 5 I also discuss the effect of the various individual strategies on individual satisfaction or happiness. In the final chapter, I will take a more in depth look at public policies towards returnees, the extent to which they meet the needs of returnees, their shortcomings, and how these can be remedied in order to help returnees be more successful.

RELATIVELY POSITIVE SOCIAL CONTEXTS

Societal attitudes towards returnees vary widely historically and culturally. In some cases, attitudes are relatively positive. I use the word "relatively" because I have found that in most cases, returnees face some negativity even if the context is generally positive.

A case of a positive social context is the situation faced by first responders to the 9/11 attacks on the World Trade Center—the hundreds of firefighters, police, medical workers, construction workers, and others who rushed to the scene and labored there for many days, weeks, and months to rescue survivors, recover bodies, and clean up debris. A quote from Benjamin J. Luft's introduction to a collection of oral histories, *We're Not Leaving: 9/11 Responders Tell Their Stories of Courage, Sacrifice and Renewal*, expresses the kind of respect and admiration with which the first responders have been greeted in the United States:

> The rest of us have much to learn from the responders about the many aspects of human behavior when called to serve in response to a disaster. We see them as the generous and altruistic heroes that they are: men and women who faced violence and horror for the sake of the greater good, men and women who risked their own lives for others, who do not see themselves as heroes, but rather humbly tell stories of the bravery and courage of *others*. We learn that the substance of who we are as Americans is not defined solely by our government and institutions; it is ultimately defined by the character and actions of our people. It is something to be proud of (2011: xxi).

In that last sentence, the returnees are seen as extraordinary, yet subsumed under the umbrella of Americans; they are exemplars of the best in all of us rather than people to be held at arm's length. Luft organized the oral history project together with colleagues at the World Trade Medical Monitoring and Treatment Center Clinic in Islandia, New York, where over 6,000 responders have received health care for over a decade. Approximately 125 people were interviewed, during a period of eighteen months. Luft and his team sought to honor the first responders, to help them in their healing process, and to help all Americans "come to terms with" the disaster of 9/11.

Despite all the positivity, this project is a good example of the "relativity" of the generally positive societal attitude toward the first responders. When Luft first sought to set up a volunteer-based clinic to help meet both medical and emotional needs, "politics, avarice and fear set roadblocks on our path." Ultimately the clinic came into existence with the help of labor leaders, local volunteer fire departments, and donors. Many first responders became angry and disillusioned at "how they were treated by a society that dragged its feet in responding to their needs when they became ill as a result of responding to the disaster" (Luft 2011: xii, xviii, xx, xxi). In 2010, Congress created a $2.8 billion fund for compensation to first responders for ailments caused by exposure to the toxic air and debris, and loss of income due to inability to work. People must prove that they were actually on the scene in order to be eligible, something that official first responders can usually do more easily than the many unofficial volunteers who were allowed to help in the "exposure zone." Years later, such unofficial volunteers were still struggling for compensation (Hartocollis 2013).

Another case of a relatively positive social context is the reception of Holocaust survivors in the U.S. after World War II. At that time, 140,000 Holocaust survivors emigrated from Europe and other places to the United States (and another 37,000 went to Canada). Hundreds of ships regularly crossed the Atlantic between 1946 and 1953, carrying thousands of survivors to the United States. Most entered through New York City, but they came through other cities as well: San Francisco, New Orleans, Boston, Galveston, Baltimore. As soon as they arrived here, "the survivors were generally greeted by a small army of people who were concerned about their welfare" (Helmreich 1992:29). In New York, organizations such as the Hebrew Immigrant Aid Society, United Service for New Americans, the National Council of Jewish Women, and the Traveler's Aid Society were present at the docks; the immigrants were provided with welcome boxes of food and well wishes, and were transported to hotel rooms by a fleet of drivers. A concerted effort was made to make them feel wanted (Helmreich 1992:30). Around the country, organizations such as the National Council of Jewish Women (NCJW) worked tirelessly to welcome the immigrants and to "Americanize" them. For example, according to a biography of Anne Levy, who settled in New Orleans, the NCJW Social Adjustment Committee helped families find jobs and apartments, and gave them furniture and clothing; it taught them how to shop for groceries, how to raise their children as Americans, how to dress, and how to generally "fit in." It sponsored English classes, and organized tours of New Orleans. (Powell 2000:380–83) Young survivors found teachers, mentors, scholarships, and fellowships when they entered American schools and colleges, and were soon on the fast track to becoming professionals. Some wonderful stories of this welcoming process are contained in Bernice Lerner's book, *The Triumph of Wounded Souls*, which is based on interviews with seven Holocaust survivors who had come to the United States as young people (Lerner 2004). Public policy towards the immigrants also reflected the relatively positive attitudes of Americans. Although at first, eligibility for immigration was restricted by a quota system, the Displaced Persons Act, which was passed by Congress in 1948 by a lopsidedly favorable margin, considerably upped the numbers of refugees who could enter the country. The first version of this Act favored Christians over Jews, because it favored people who had been in Germany or Austria before 1945 (excluding perhaps 150,000 Jews who had fled pogroms in Poland and gone there in 1946), as well as applicants from the Baltic nations and farmers, few of whom were Jewish. However, President Truman was highly supportive of a campaign to remove the restrictions, and in 1950 signed an amended version of the Act that was much more favorable to Holocaust survivors (Helmreich 1992:47–48).

The treatment of Holocaust survivors is another example of the "relativity" of a generally positive societal attitude toward returnees. In a fascinating book, *Case Closed: Holocaust Survivors in Postwar America,* Beth B. Cohen (2007) reported on her detailed research into how relief agencies handled the cases of the Holocaust survivors they were assisting. These agencies were primarily based in the American Jewish community and supported through fundraising campaigns. They sponsored a sizeable percentage of the Holocaust survivors coming to the United States, and also assisted those sponsored by individuals when the individual sponsors proved unable to provide sufficient help. Sponsorship entailed guaranteeing that the refugee would have housing and a job. By reading agency documents and conducting interviews, Cohen discovered that with some exceptions, agency policies and staff showed a lack of sensitivity to the survivors' psychological and social needs. For example, in a rush to close cases before a one-year time limit was up, people were pushed to take any available jobs without much consideration for their prior education or professions, or trauma-induced illnesses. Clients were also pushed to settle in cities they had no desire to go to. Religious functionaries (rabbis, seminary students, ritual slaughterers, cantors) were encouraged to take available jobs rather than to continue in their religious statuses. The agencies saw their goal as enabling the refugees to achieve self-sufficiency, a strong American value. This seems to have hindered their ability to give full attention to individual situations.

NEGATIVE SOCIAL CONTEXTS

In other cases, societal attitudes are hostile, even punitive. A good example is the situation faced by Americans who left the American Communist Party during the 1950s. More than a million Americans had joined the Communist

Party at one time or another during the first half of the twentieth century. They left in great numbers in the wake of Khrushchev's revelations about the crimes of Stalin. Within a few weeks after Khrushchev's report, 30,000 people had left, and in about a year, the Party had dwindled to be more like what it had been in 1919 when it was just founded. The exodus from the Party came just at the time that the Party was being persecuted during the McCarthy "witchhunts." Communist or ex-Communist became a kind of negative master status. Vivian Gornick pointed out in *The Romance of American Communism* that during the McCarthy period, Communists "were hunted like criminals, suffered trial and imprisonment, endured social isolation and loss of work, had their professional lives destroyed, and, in the case of the Rosenbergs, were put to death." An actress Gornick interviewed spoke about her years struggling to get work when she had been blacklisted by the theater industry. The actress had been called to testify before the House Un-American Activities Committee, and taken the Fifth Amendment. She felt that after that "I was no longer an American." Potential employers were never up front about the blacklist. Instead, she would go for an audition, be told she was hired, and then the next morning she would get a call saying that there had been a mistake, e.g., the show was being postponed. Later she would find that someone else had been hired. She went to Europe for three years because Europeans were willing to hire blacklisted American actors (Gornick 1977:10, 232).

Former Communists also faced hostility from those who had remained in the Party. Members had often been put on trial and expelled for challenging the Party's ideology, strategies, or rules. After expulsion, they would be shunned by those still in the Party. Those who voluntarily left the Party faced similar treatment. Gornick interviewed a woman who had left the Party in 1958, not quite realizing what this would mean for her relationships with friends and acquaintances within the Party. "I had become—literally over-night—nonexistent. The only people who remained our friends were the people who quit with us: at the same moment, over the same issues. Everyone else disappeared. People stopped calling, stopped dropping by, crossed the street when we ran into each other" (Gornick 1977: 177).

Another example of hostile and punitive societal attitudes is the situation faced by former prisoners in the United States, especially those who come from working class and racial/ethnic minority backgrounds. Some want ads tell the story:

"No arrests or convictions of any kind for the past seven years. No Felony arrests or convictions of any kind for life." (Job ad for electrician contractor) "We are looking for people with . . . spotless background/criminal history." (Job ad for warehouse worker or delivery drivers) "ALL CANDIDATES WILL BE E-VERIFIED AND MUST CLEAR A BACKGROUND CHECK

(NO PRIORS)" (Job ad for manufacturing jobs) (from a study by the National
Employment Law Project, quoted in Alexander 2012:153).

As is well known, there has been a huge growth in the number of Americans
incarcerated since the 1970s, with over 2 million people in prison at the time
of this writing. The U.S. today has the highest incarceration rate per capita of
any industrialized country. The term "mass incarceration" is increasingly
used to characterize the United States prison system. Nations in the democratic, industrial world tend to incarcerate *violent* criminals at about the same
rate as the U.S. The U.S. is set apart due to how it treats property and drug
crimes. These crimes began to be treated more and more harshly after the
1970s. Around 77 percent of the growth in the prison population in the period
1978–1996 was accounted for by nonviolent offenders, especially drug offenders, whose numbers grew eleven times during the period. As a result,
around one in every 109 U.S. males and one in every 1,695 females were
incarcerated by the year 2000. Since so many are incarcerated, there is a
large stream of prisoners eventually being released into the community: over
600,000 prisoners are released from U.S. Federal and State prisons every
year. Rates of incarceration are not equal across the lines of gender, race, and
class. As the statistic above indicates, prisoners and ex-prisoners are mainly
male. Most prisoners are from low income backgrounds, and about two-
thirds of returning prisoners are racial or ethnic minorities, with African
Americans being the largest number (Petersilia 2003:3, 21–22, 26–30).

It is beyond the scope of this book to examine the *origins* of this astonish-
ing development of mass incarceration, but a short list of circumstances
researchers have identified, as discussed by Michelle Alexander in *The New
Jim Crow*, includes: deindustrialization, which deprived millions of young
men without college degrees or steady jobs; the rise of the drug trade, which
provided jobs and coincided with deindustrialization; the perception of threat
felt by many whites as manufacturing jobs declined and African-Americans
began to take advantage of gains made during the Civil Rights era; conservative politicians in both the Republican and Democratic Parties catering to the
white backlash, in order to gain power; the associated rise of the punitive
"law and order" movement and "War on Drugs" which catered to white
backlash sentiments; and treating the drug trade as a law enforcement rather
than a public health problem (Alexander 2012:40–58). Over time, systemic
racism in the "War on Drugs" has perpetuated mass incarceration of African
Americans. For example, law enforcement against the drug trade has been
focused on communities of color; there are few significant constraints on the
use of police discretion in searches and seizures, as the courts have allowed
the Fourth Amendment and other civil rights to be undermined in order to
achieve increased drug arrests; and racial profiling is rampant (Alexander
2012:59–96, 130–36).

Contrary to what many Americans have been encouraged to think, prisons are not a "country club" culture, but extraordinary cultures in which "rehabilitation," once the goal of American prisons, has been replaced by punishment and deterrence. Only a minority of prisoners exiting from prison have been able to participate in job training or educational programs. In 1994, Congress eliminated Pell grants for prisoners with the result that "prison college programs are virtually extinct in most states." Only 13 percent of released prisoners have participated in any sort of pre-release education program. In the 1990s, state legislators and prison administrators eliminated various privileges and programs that once existed. Targeted were the ability to smoke, use weight lifting equipment, hot meals, personal clothing, phone calls, family days, etc. People leaving this situation return to the community not well positioned to lead an ordinary life free from crime (Petersilia 2004:4–5).

To make things worse, the hostile and punitive attitudes associated with the War on Drugs follow the formerly incarcerated as they return. Former prisoners have great difficulty finding jobs, as the job ads quoted earlier indicate. Most states allow employers to discriminate on the basis of past criminal convictions. Jobs usually available to people without a lot of education, such as manufacturing jobs, have long ago left the cities in favor of the suburbs, so these are not available to ex-prisoners without automobiles, even if an employer would hire them. In addition to unemployment, former prisoners often face homelessness. Housing discrimination against convicted felons is "routine," according to Alexander, by both public and private landlords. Federal law actually authorizes public housing authorities to refuse to rent to drug offenders and other felons. Newly released prisoners also face large debts, in the form of payments required for drug testing, various pre-conviction service fees (e.g., jail book-in fees), and post-conviction service fees (e.g., public defender recoupment fees, fees for residential or work-release programs). Child support debts accumulate during incarceration and must be faced upon release. The welfare reform legislation initiated in 1996 under President Clinton requires that states permanently bar individuals with drug-related felony convictions from receiving Federal aid under the Temporary Assistance for Needy Families program (TANF). They can also be barred from receiving food stamps. Former prisoners also lose voting rights: the majority of states do not allow felons to vote while on parole. Some states deny the right to vote even after that, for terms ranging from a few years to life (Alexander 2012:144–60; Petersilia 2003:116–26, 130–36). Finally, there is a huge shame and stigma associated with having been a prisoner. "One may learn to cope with the stigma of criminality, but like the stigma of race, the prison label is not something that a black man in the ghetto can ever fully escape" (Alexander 2012:162). The two works just cited reflect that today there is a growing movement originating within communities of color to change this negative treatment, and growing attention in the criminal justice field to the problem of "re-entry." There has been some positive response by government, especially with regard to nonviolent offenders. Some states have begun to implement changes, and in 2015, President Obama called for reform of the criminal justice system. At the time of this writing, it is not yet clear whether these trends can break the entrenched hostile societal attitudes that have prevailed since the 1970s.

AMBIVALENT SOCIAL CONTEXTS

In some cases societal attitudes are mixed rather than being mostly negative or positive, as in the cases discussed above. When a country has been politically divided, and the extraordinary experiences are connected to political conflicts that have not been completely resolved, the reception given to those who return home reflects the ambivalent political situation. The reception given to Vietnam veterans is of course the iconic example for the United States. The country was divided on Vietnam, and returning Vietnam veterans were praised by some and condemned by others. For example, stories of returning Vietnam veterans being spat upon by anti-war protestors have circulated down through the decades since the war. This kind of highly negative treatment may not really have been as widespread as commonly thought. Jerry Lembcke, in *The Spitting Image: Myth, Memory and the Legacy of Vietnam.* provides a good deal of evidence for his argument that it is a myth that functions to uphold conservative views on the war (1998). But the story is persistent and has the power to evoke emotions among soldiers and veterans and their families. Americans today are careful to separate anti-war sentiments from anti-soldier sentiments. One poster from the Peace Movement during the war in Iraq read "Support the Troops, End the War." Today's returning troops face contradictions: they may be greeted by the public with a "thank you for your service," but at the same time face an uphill struggle for medical care, jobs, and housing. The struggle of American veterans for such resources will be discussed in the next chapter.

An example of ambivalence toward returnees that is less well known in the U.S. is the treatment of members of the French resistance who had been arrested by the Vichy regime and turned over to the Nazis. Tens of thousands resistance members met this fate, of whom 40,760 came home after the war, 8,872 of those women. In *A Train in Winter,* Caroline Moorehead has told the story of 230 women involved in the resistance who were taken to Nazi concentration camps, along with some 31,000 others in the spring of 1942. Of the 230 only thirty-nine returned, after experiencing unspeakable horrors in camps such as Auschwitz, Birkenau, Ravensbruck, and Mauthausen. Resisters who could prove French nationality, termed *politiques*, were given better entitlements than those who couldn't, termed *raciales.* The *politiques* received 5,000 francs, extra food rations, and a long paid holiday. Some of the women were asked to testify at war crimes trials. But according to Moorehead,

> France was not altogether in the mood to hear what they had to say . . . De Gaulle, pushing his myth of France as a country of united resisters betrayed by a handful of traitors, needed collective amnesia. The gaunt, sickly deportees were an unwelcome reminder that in five weeks the Germans had crushed what had been considered one of the finest armies in the world; and that, during four years of occupation, it was the French themselves who had rounded up and interned Jews and resisters, before sending them to their death in Poland (Moorehead 2011:303–4).

Perhaps not unsurprisingly, women resisters received less attention than men, with the exception of Danielle Casanova, a Communist heroine who became a symbol of resistance and had streets and babies named after her. Of the 1,053 resisters who received the honor of the *Compagnons de la Liberation* only six were women. Armed combat was in keeping with de Gaulle's image of the resisters, and the roles played by women as "messengers, couriers, printers, distributors of banned literature, providers of safe houses, did not seem quite heroic enough" (Moorehead 2011:303–4).

Another case of national ambivalence is the situation of *Gulag* survivors in the former Soviet Union. People arrested for political opposition under the reign of Stalin and his successors ended up in prisons known as the *Gulag*. It has been estimated that from eight to twelve million political prisoners labored in these camps between 1929 and 1956, starving and freezing, dying of malnutrition, exposure, and disease. The government began to release a trickle of them in the later 1940s, mostly people who had been given determinate sentences that had ended. But in the 1950s when Khrushchev's regime began to criticize the human rights abuses of Stalinism, millions of prisoners (called *zeks*) were released and began to return home. In the backlash against Khrushchev, this slowed, but resumed again under Gorbachev, and millions more were still being released into the 1990s after the dissolution of the Soviet Union. They faced a difficult situation. The leaders of the Soviet system, including Khrushchev himself, feared that de-Stalinization would destabilize the entire system. The same was true of lower level Communist Party members and State officials. Too many people had a vested interest in Stalinist programs, policies, and decisions, and the presence of former prisoners with believable claims of innocence would serve as a threat to their economic and political privileges—including apartments, positions, dachas, etc. taken from the arrestees (Adler 2004:17–29, 31–33). The debate over Stalin continues to this day in Russia. To many, Stalin is still portrayed as a hero, responsible for leading the country to industrialization, great power status, and victory over the Nazis in World War II. Crimes that may have been committed have either been exaggerated, or are less important than the achievements of the Stalinist system. But many others see Stalin as the symbol of human rights abuses, totalitarianism, elitism, and a dysfunctional economic system that stifled individual initiative and creativity. Thus it is not surprising that *Gulag* survivors released during the 1940s and the Khrushchev period, along with a welcome home, also faced a political climate fraught with official hostility toward them. Some of the prisoners "released" in the 1940s found themselves re-arrested, tried for the same "crime," and sentenced to exile ("permanent settlement") in remote regions such as eastern Siberia or Kazakhstan. A directive prohibited supervisors from giving former prisoners good jobs. Professionals who worked in fields such as teaching and journalism found it impossible to get work in their fields. Even under Khrushchev, release did not automatically mean "rehabilitation," defined by Khrushchev as "revision of all legal consequences of a judgment pertaining to a person who was unlawfully prosecuted, in consequence of the acknowledgement of innocence." Rehabilitation was granted after a lengthy review process, and was recognized in the form of a certificate. Some were declared "rehabilitated," but under condition that they never speak about the situations they faced in the *Gulag*. Some had charges against them dropped, but were exiled to remote Siberia or Kazakhstan, far from their homes. Some were forbidden to be closer than 101 kilometers to Moscow, Leningrad, Kiev, and other big cities. Some were re-sentenced into psychiatric institutions. Former prisoners had a notation regarding their imprisonment in the work books citizens had to carry, which meant that they were barred from better jobs. Their previous apartments were not restored to them, and it was difficult to find new housing (Adler 2004: 57–63, 99, 152–68). Many tried to re-join, or join, the Communist Party, either because they still believed in it, or because it was a way to getting a better job, apartment, pension, and other State benefits. Only half who applied were accepted (Adler 2004:29, 63; Applebaum 2003:519–20). Even the officially exonerated felt insecure after Khrushchev's ouster. Some were told by officials "The rehabilitated are no longer in fashion," or "Far too many were rehabilitated" (Cohen 2010:132).

A final case of national ambivalence is the situation of people in the U.S. who have been released from prison after *exoneration*. Since 1973, 138 people have been exonerated of capital crimes and released from prison after spending an average of nearly ten years on death row. Another 273 have been exonerated of other crimes based on DNA evidence after spending an average of thirteen years in prison. Innocent death row inmates have suffered an experience that is highly traumatic. They face death, knowing that it is undeserved and wrongful, on top of all the other difficulties faced by inmates in general. Sociologists Saundra D. Westervelt and Kimberly J. Cook did indepth interviews with eighteen exonerated death row inmates for their book *Life After Death Row* (2012:3). They found that upon release, half of their respondents felt "welcomed and accepted" by their communities. However a third felt stigmatized. The acceptance stories are heartwarming. Walter McMillian, for example, returned to his hometown of Monroeville, Alabama, after release. McMillan told Westervelt and Cook that he returned to a town that supported him and treated him with dignity. "'I think I get the whole community for support because everybody treat me just like they did before I got locked up, or better . . . So I am blessed.'" McMillian described how people helped him get back on his feet and get a business established. He recounted an instance when men working for the county helped him clear gravel from his driveway free of charge, and he explained with a smile that he is greeted warmly by officials at the courthouse whenever he goes there to do business (Westervelt and Cook 2012:175–77). However, interviewees who were stigmatized told some chilling stories. Kirk Bloodworth returned to a small town on Maryland's eastern shore after being exonerated by DNA evidence of having murdered a nine year old girl. He suffered a hundred incidents of being treated like a pariah. People called him "child killer," slammed the door in his face when he knocked looking for work, grabbed their children when he walked near them at the supermarket, and wrote "child killer," "murderer," and "rapist" on his car. For a time, he was homeless and living out of his car (Westervelt and Cook 2012:180–81). The ambivalence in American society about exonerated inmates is expressed in the paucity of support for them upon release. According to Westervelt and Cook, only 27 states provide monetary compensation, and only 10 provide help with housing, employment, or education. In some states the exonerated cannot access services provided to parolees, even though they have been in prison for lengthy periods of time and need these services just as much as non-exonerated inmates (Westervelt and Cook 2012:200). And almost nowhere do the exonerated get what they feel they need the most in order to recover from trauma: "recognition of the wrong done to them and acknowledgment of their status as an innocent person. They want their wrongful conviction made visible for all to see and their reputation restored" (Westervelt and Cook 2012:195). The reluctance to compensate becomes symbolic for the government's failure to take responsibility. First, the government wrongfully convicts and traumatizes them, then it expects the exonerated to cope with the aftermath "on their own" or solely with the help of sympathetic family, friends, and struggling nonprofit agencies (Westervelt and Cook 2012:206–8).

FAMILY CONTEXTS

Now let us turn from the national setting to the more intimate worlds of family and community. How are families affected when one member leaves for an extraordinary experience, and later returns? What kinds of reception do returnees get from their families? Again, situations vary widely, historically and cross-culturally.

In some cases, where returnees face a societal stigma, families are tainted by the same stigma as the returnees and suffer negative consequences simply because they are related to the person who had the extraordinary experience. In the Soviet Union during Stalin's reign, there were millions of "wives and children of traitors to the Motherland," who suffered because they were related to someone persecuted as an "enemy of the people" (Cohen 2010:28–29). Some wives and children of "enemies of the people" were imprisoned and executed. If a wife were to denounce her husband, she might be able to avoid this. Divorce was encouraged by making the fees cheaper for the spouses of those who had been sent to the *Gulag* (Adler 2004: 63–64). The widow of Nikolai Bukharin, a founding leader of the Soviet Union executed by Stalin as an "enemy of the people," spent two decades in prisons, labor camps, and Siberian exile; the couple's child was separated from the mother and grew up in an orphanage without being told who his parents were. As many as four to five million children may have been sent to the *Gulag* along with a family member, or ended up in orphanages (Cohen 2010:28–30). Some children who were free lived with extended family members or a parent who was not sent away, but their lives were marked by loneliness, visits to a parent in prison, or discrimination in education and job assignments (Frierson: 2015). The adult relatives who managed to avoid death or incarceration lived repressed lives. Some managed to hide their connections with the accused relative. But it was difficult to avoid discrimination. When applying for a job, an apartment, etc. relatives were usually asked to reveal information about immediate family members (Cohen 2010:28–30).

The families of prisoners in America's drug war may not suffer such severe repression. However, they do face profound stigmatization. Donald Braman studied families affected by mass incarceration in Washington, D.C. Through extensive ethnographic research, he found that not only the prisoners but also their family members were hurt and stigmatized by their status (Braman 2004). According to Michelle Alexander, Braman's and other studies have shown that families often maintain a silence about a member's incarceration. "Imprisonment is seen as so shameful that many people avoid talking about it, even within their own families." Families may also lie about a member's incarceration in an effort to mitigate the stigma. The result, according to Michelle Alexander, is a kind of "collective denial of lived experience." Pretending that it isn't happening, family members deny themselves the support and comfort they might get from others going through the same troubles (Alexander 2010:165–69).

In addition to family victimization or stigmatization, returnees may not return to an intact family or community situation. The family may have broken down as a result of the family member's departure. Or family members may reject the returnee because they took the other side in a conflict. In cases of disasters, revolution, and war, families may have fled or been killed. We have seen this above, in the cases of Nando Parrado, Ishmael Beah, and Anita Schorr.

Family breakdown may be a direct or indirect consequence of the family member's departure for the extraordinary experience. In the case of American prisoners, in addition to stigmatization, imprisonment often contributes to family disruption. After a father is imprisoned, the family often has to move into smaller living quarters; the mother, having to seek more employment, has less time to spend on childrearing; and a new man may join the family. After a mother is imprisoned, children are often taken in by relatives rather than remaining with the father. The punitive measures exercised against prisoners in recent decades have included limiting the number of visits by family members. More than ten million American children have a parent who was incarcerated at some point in the child's life. A parent's imprisonment is known to be a traumatizing event for a child. This can be mitigated by maintaining regular contact. However, in a Bureau of Justice study, 54 percent of female prisoners reported that they had no personal visits with their children since admission. Deterrents to visitation, in addition to prison restrictions, include geographical distance, lack of transportation, and the inability of a child's caregiver to bring the child to the prison during visiting hours. The major method of contact with imprisoned family members is by U.S. mail, followed by telephone; personal visits are the least likely. An obstacle to frequent phone calls also exists: most states only allow inmates to make collect calls, which are very expensive. When an inmate is in prison for a long period of time, all of these forms of contact decline (Petersilia 2003:42–46, 227–28).

As we saw above in the case of Stalin's reign, political conflict in the Soviet Union led some people to denounce a family member who had been targeted as an "enemy of the people." Returnees who had been denounced by their families returned to the ordinary world as isolated individuals. A similar situation faced some participants in America's Civil Rights Movement, both African American and white. Joan C. Browning was a young white girl from the rural South who became involved in the Civil Rights Movement as a college student at Georgia State College for Women. She was first forced to leave college due to her activities. As Browning's involvement with the Civil Rights Movement deepened, she also became estranged from her family. Her parents divorced, and her father stopped staying in touch. Her mother remarried. Her mother was not against integration, and she made it clear that she loved Browning, but she feared that she and the other six children would be harassed if she did not break with her. Browning wrote:

> Being "written out of my family" has scarred and shaped my life ever since. It was immediately horrible. I did not yet have a fully formed identity apart from my place in my family, so I literally did not know who I was . . . I experienced a lifelong separation from my large and loving family . . . for me, and for many other women like me, participation made us outcasts—women without a home (Curry et al. 2000:71–72, 82).

Families of African American people who joined the Movement sometimes pressured them to drop out, fearing that they or other family members would be killed. When John Reynolds joined the Movement in Alabama as a young man, his father beat him and said, "You're not my son anymore." Eventually they reconciled, and his father was proud of Reynolds for his courage and sense of purpose (Reynolds 2012:26–27, 103).

Survivors of extraordinary experiences in religious groups face a variety of family situations upon exiting. Some return to an intact and loving family that missed them and is happy to have them home. The family may even have gone so far as to hire deprogrammers to detain and persuade them to return home. Other returnees face the opposite situation: they have left, while their family has remained in the group. Complicated situations exist, as well, in which some family members are in, and others out. Returnees who leave family behind may face troubling circumstances. Some groups banish those who leave, prohibiting family members who are still inside from having any contact with them. Lauren Drain left the Westboro Baptist Church, which her parents had joined when she was a child. Her parents, and a brother and sister had stayed in. Drain was a nurse and had found a job working in a hospital after she left. One day she ran into her father at the hospital. "I did a double take when I saw him. He looked me straight in the eye, then turned around and walked away. He wasn't even courteous enough to acknowledge me. I was a nurse, a person, and his daughter. He looked at me with an expression that let me know that I was not even human in his eyes" (Drain 2013:272). Drain would call her mother or father but the calls were usually rejected. Once she called her father on his birthday to wish him a happy birthday. He said, "I don't know why you're calling me . . . I enjoyed my time with you, but we are done now. I don't really know what else we have to say" (Drain 2013:275). Jenna Miscavige's parents joined Scientology when she was a small child. They had been brought into the group by her father's father, Ron Miscavige. Jenna's parents became members of the group's ruling group, Sea Org. Her uncle, David Miscavige, became the group's leader after its founder, L. Ron Hubbard, died. When Jenna Miscavige became a young adult, her parents left the Sea Org, although they did not leave the organization altogether. Jenna Miscavige subsequently decided to leave altogether, concerned about the group's coercive and abusive treatment of its members. Her grandparents left sometime later. The family was in turmoil throughout the period that the various members were disengaging from Scientology. David Miscivige, the uncle, was actively involved in trying to manipulate Jenna Miscavige's parents into staying in Sea Org. After they left, it seems they never spoke with him again. David Miscavige was also involved in trying to control Jenna Miscavige's exit arrangements (Hill 2013:387–92).

Such religious group experiences feature extreme situations of family conflict facing returnees, but family conflict can occur in a more subtle way as well. Mark Alessi, the aid worker described in the previous chapter, usually returns to the U.S. to visit his family of origin when he is in between contracts. Alessi has several siblings and an elderly parent who has begun to exhibit symptoms of dementia. According to Alessi, his family are often "down on me" because they do not believe he is doing a fair share of care for the parent. They do not seem to appreciate that he had built 350 houses in Africa while he was gone, or that he had helped numerous street children and former child soldiers have an opportunity to live lives in the mainstream. Once he was even told to stop visiting for more than a couple of days, as family members said it was too stressful for them. Fortunately, Alessi has an alternative support network of more like-minded American friends with whom he built relationships years ago before he began his career overseas.

PUBLIC POLICY

Finally, let us consider the question of public policy—programs to help returnees come back to the ordinary world. Until recently, even when societal attitudes were favorable to returnees, helpful re-entry programs rarely existed or were confined to assistance with practical and material matters, such as housing, education, and work, without dealing with issues of the self and identity, including emotional trauma. For example, it is well known that after World War II, there was a sort of national determination in the U.S. to adopt a cheerful and optimistic stance of going forward.

In recent years there has been a growing awareness of need for public policies in country after country, and on the level of international bodies like the United Nations. Attention to the issue has been forced by social movements and the sheer numbers of people returning from extraordinary experiences. I will return to the question of public policy and discuss it in more depth in chapter 6.

UNANSWERED QUESTIONS

The topics explored in this chapter on contexts of return does not exhaust the possible topics that could be covered. The economic context would be an interesting topic to explore. For example, volunteers in the Civil Rights Movement returned to a job market that was less than favorable. Young people who were born around the same time as the activists—during and just after World War II—but who were *not* politically active entered the labor market in the mid to late 1960s. They faced abundant opportunities due to an economic boom and a shortage of workers. Civil rights volunteers who postponed their entrance into the job market until the 1970s had a harder time findings jobs, and their incomes never caught up with those of non-activists over the course of their lifetimes (McAdam 1988:211, 224–28). I hope future researchers will take up the topic of the economic context.

Another interesting topic is the phenomenon of people who enter and exit in groups from extraordinary situations. Such situations are worthy of special attention, for they have dynamics of their own that deserve to be explored in detail. An example is the town of Buffalo Creek, West Virginia, which experienced a devastating flood in 1972. Survivors continued to live on in the same town, yet the communal culture of the town had been utterly destroyed by the events. In his classic study, Kai T. Erikson, characterized this loss of community as "collective trauma" and explored the ways in which this collective trauma heightened the individual traumas of the people in the town. Unlike the cases covered in this book, returnees were not making a return to an ordinary world that had continued more or less intact while returnees were away. Their situation seems more akin to the one I described in the Introduction, of survivors of war, plague, or famine in ancient times continuing on amongst themselves as best they could after the troubles lifted. Buffalo Creek's culture had been centered on close knit neighborhoods. When the physical structures were destroyed, the government assigned survivors to live in thirteen mobile home camps, without consideration for keeping neighbors together. The survivors were united in feelings of loneliness for a neighborly culture that was forever gone (Erikson 1976:153–55).

Another example is the context of some demobilized combatants after civil wars. Former soldiers may have originally become combatants as members of groups, such as villagers who join a revolutionary force for protection against government violence. Through an officially sponsored demobilization process, they may then return to the ordinary world in groups rather than as isolated individuals. And demobilization arrangements may ensure that they remain in groups, such as resettlement camps or new villages. In El Salvador, for example, after the peace settlement, FMLN guerrillas and supporters were often settled into villages to take part in a peasant farm economy on newly redistributed land. The FMLN maintained a presence and former guerrillas and supporters whose wartime roles had equipped them with skills useful in peacetime often became political officials or other kinds of community leaders. On the other hand, El Salvador's returnees seem to have experienced a certain pervasive presence of the "ordinary" in the form of cultural traditions (such as gender roles) that persisted both during and after the war, and in the form of interactions with people representing national government, international and local aid agencies, etc. (Viterna 2013).

For now, let us go on to explore the challenges faced by returnees and the strategies they typically use to meet these challenges. Regardless of social context, I have found that there are great similarities, in both challenges faced, and how returnees typically deal with them.

Chapter Four

The Challenges of Returning to the Ordinary World

No matter how diverse the experiences may have been, there are some common challenges faced by individuals returning to the ordinary world after extraordinary experiences. These are challenges to meeting some of the most basic needs that all human beings have. Those who meet the challenges successfully seem to have a better chance for a happy and satisfying life after their return. In this chapter, I turn to an examination of five typical challenges I have identified through my reading and interviews.

The first challenge is to meet the need for survival: to establish material security and safety for oneself. Not everyone faces this challenge—for example, a soldier from a middle class family returning to the U.S. from Afghanistan may return to the shelter of a parental home—but for many returnees, this is a paramount challenge, fraught with uncertainty and obstacles. The second challenge is to learn or re-learn how to go about daily life in the culture of the ordinary world. For people who have been away for a long time, there may be many changes to adjust to, including proper patterns of communication, technology, even changes on the important level of values and beliefs. The third challenge is to reconstruct one's sense of self and identity. Having been transformed by the extraordinary experience, a person cannot simply go back to being who they were before. Aspects of the self and identity that originated and developed during the extraordinary experience may not function very well in the new context, and will have to be shed or reworked. The fourth challenge, closely connected to the third, is to reinterpret or fit the extraordinary experience into one's evolving ideas about what gives life meaning and purpose. Perhaps the meaning one gave to the experience while engaged in it may not survive when a person returns to the ordinary world. Or perhaps the opposite may be the case, the meaning one gave to the experience while engaged in it may in some way carry over to ordinary life. The fifth challenge, also closely connected to the previous two, is to develop new, satisfying relationships with others, and renew old relationships in a way that will be satisfying.

A note on why I have chosen this idea of challenges. Sometimes the process of returning to an ordinary life has been seen, not as a set of challenges, but as a stage or a series of stages that are gone through (e.g., for recovering from trauma, see Herman 1992: 233 ff.). The idea of stages implies that the return to an ordinary life is a kind of liminal state, meaning a stage or period between two periods, past and future, which a returnee eventually gets through. When I began my research, I initially thought about the process in terms of stages. But the more I explored the topic, the more I realized that a sort of linear set of stages did not match what I was seeing in the memoirs and interviews. I also discovered several authors who criticized the idea of stages or insightfully utilized the idea of challenges in discussing transitions from an extraordinary or different situation to a more ordinary life. Ebaugh, in *Becoming an Ex*, characterized the entire process of exiting from a role as a series of stages, but discussed the final stage, or formation of the "ex" identity, in terms of a series of challenges. (Ebaugh 1988) The notion of change as a "circular" or "spiral" process has also been brought up by John Paul Lederach and Angela Jill Lederach in *When Blood and Bones Cry Out,* a book about healing and reconciliation after wars and genocidal conflicts (2010). They point out that the discourse on reconciliation in international aid agencies tends to be framed in terms of a linear process of steps, phases, or stages, through which individuals and groups progress to a better situation. However, in their own experiences working with communities of survivors in Africa and Central America, the process is really more like a spiral or circle. According to the Lederachs "a phase based understanding captured in prevalent linguistic terms like pre-conflict, post-conflict, post-accord, post-violence, post-war" cannot completely capture the situation of people living amidst *ongoing* insecurity, displacement, and voicelessness, brought on by continued violent attacks and/or structural violence in the form of poverty, lack of access to clean water and healthcare, and human rights abuses" (Lederach and Lederach 2010:48, 50). The notion of a "spiral" was also utilized by Karen Armstrong (2004) in her memoir of her life after leaving a Roman Catholic convent in England.

The idea of the return process as a set of challenges also implies that the challenges themselves are not linear. For many people they are *simultaneous* in nature; a person may be confronting all of them at the same time. Or they may be *repetitive;* a person may confront a challenge successfully at one point in time, only to face it again at a later point in life (Prochaska, Norcross et al. 1994). There is also a dimension of *depth;* a person may partially meet a challenge at one level, and return to it later to deal with it more completely.

THE FIRST CHALLENGE: SURVIVAL

By "survival" I mean meeting material needs for food, clothing, shelter, medical care, and also meeting needs for safety or security from bodily or psychological harm. For returnees who do not come back to a comfortable home and family, material survival and safety is a priority. Survivors of trauma, in particular, need to establish a sense of safety. In some situations, this is made all the more difficult by the continuation of extraordinary circumstances—for example, as the Lederachs brought up, people who escape genocidal attacks may end up in refugee camps that are still periodically under attack from their enemies.

The stories of two child survivors of the Holocaust whom I interviewed illustrate just how preoccupied some returnees must be with meeting immediate survival needs. Anita Schorr, whose story I began to tell in an earlier chapter, survived Auschwitz and other forced labor situations, and was freed at the age of fifteen with no family, home, or community to return to. Her mother and younger brother had been murdered at Auschwitz. Her father survived most of the war years at Auschwitz, only to be shot and killed two days before the war was over. After being freed, Schorr first stayed in a military hospital until she was physically well enough to move on. She then went to Prague, a beautiful, historic city in her home country of Czechoslovakia. She told me that she was there for two years but "never saw the buildings," she was so preoccupied with establishing herself in her new surroundings. She was also so preoccupied with survival that she could not even mourn the loss of her parents. The other child Holocaust survivor I interviewed, Eva Lukacs, was also preoccupied with survival, together with her family. Over 600,000 Jewish people in their country had been killed. Lukacs' parents were alive, but her father had lost his business. He started a smaller-scale business, but then the country's new Communist government socialized the business. Soon "enemies of the people" were being rounded up by the regime—members of the intelligentsia and many Jews. Her father then got a job with a Jewish agency that was communicating with Israeli diplomats in an effort to get help. As a result, he was imprisoned and tortured. Her father was eventually freed after Stalin's death, but returned home, in Lukacs' view, a man who had been "destroyed" physically and mentally.

Around the world today, people freed from the extraordinary experience of slavery face obstacles to material survival. The Anti-Slavery Movement has revealed that as many as 27 million people are enslaved today. Forms of slavery that are extraordinary experiences as defined in this book include: debt bondage; contract slavery, in which workers are offered a contract but find themselves working for nothing and held against their will; forced prostitution; domestic service by enslaved children; and war slavery in which governments force people to labor in support of military campaigns or on construction projects. People who become slaves are usually the poorest and most vulnerable people in the world. When they become free, whether by their own efforts, or intervention by activists or governments, they risk re-enslavement if they cannot find a way to survive. A historic example of this issue is the period after the Civil War when the U.S. government failed to fulfill the promise to give former slaves "forty acres and a mule:" the absence of resources made former slaves vulnerable to near-slavery conditions of exploitation as sharecroppers in the Jim Crow South. In addition to share-cropping, former slaves in the South who were imprisoned for petty "crimes" were contracted out to capitalist entrepreneurs to work without pay in mines and other enterprises. Today, slaves who are freed but lack resources some-times actually return to slavery out of desperation (Bales 2005:1–8, 125).

Even in countries that are affluent and peaceful, people returning from extraordinary experiences can become absorbed by trying to meet immediate material needs. In North Carolina in the 1970s, Sally Bermanzohn and her husband Paul survived a violent Ku Klux Klan attack on a peaceful civil rights march organized by the Communist Workers Party (CWP). The KKK and others fired on the marchers, while the police stood by, killing five, and wounding ten, including Paul, who was shot in the head and arm, and perma-nently disabled as a result. The Bermanzohns had both been active in the Civil Rights Movement since the 1960s and they had joined the CWP in the mid-1970s. During that period, they went through extraordinary experiences as radical activists, married, and had a daughter. They had also been pursuing higher education. Both had gone to college, and Paul Bermanzohn had grad-uated from medical school. Sally had also gone to law school before deciding that law was not the best career for her. With the CWP, they were involved in union organizing drives and other work in support of low income workers. Their activism was abruptly interrupted by the KKK attack. Their activist group was in disarray. Paul narrowly escaped death, was paralyzed on one side, and had to be preoccupied with his physical recovery. He was hospital-ized, then in rehab, and cared for, but had no medical or disability benefits from his job. Sally was preoccupied with helping Paul, caring for their small daughter, and trying to meet the family's financial needs. She had been unemployed at the time of the attack; Paul had been supporting the family with two part-time jobs. The family moved into the basement of the house of friends. Sally began to look for help: "I applied for every type of social service I could get, and I learned firsthand about America's fragmented safety net." As a woman "with no income, no savings, a child, and a totally disabled husband," she qualified for many benefits, but "to get the benefits, I needed determination, persistence, and the ability to withstand humiliation. Each program operated out of a different building and involved its own qualifications and application process. At the Welfare Department, they were suspicious of me. Who was this college-educated white woman who says she needs welfare? If I didn't have mouths to feed, I would have given up" (Bermanzohn 2003:253–54).

Schorr, Lukacs, and the Bermanzohns eventually went on to more stable, middle class lives. But not everyone does. Former prisoners in the United States, due to circumstances discussed in chapter 3, find it extremely difficult to survive after leaving prison. They face difficulties with jobs, housing, and in the absence of an adequate safety net for the homeless and unemployed, many turn to crime again in order to get money to live. As a result, many also return to prison. The recidivism rate in the United States is extremely high. Many studies have reported that around two-thirds of those released from prison are re-arrested within a few years of their release. Most of those who return to prison do so within the first year after release (Petersilia 2003:140 ff). This is a situation of people who may not be able to exit from their extraordinary prison experience, even if they want to, without some helping hands.

Some U.S. military veterans from low-income backgrounds have found themselves in a similar situation when they come home. They joined the military in the hopes of getting an education and career, and returned home with high expectations. But when they did not have a stable family home to return to, they landed on the streets, competing for jobs and housing with a growing army of the unemployed. A film, *When I Came Home*, has profiled the difficulties of one African-American veteran of the Iraq War, Herold Noel (Lohaus 2006). Sociologist Benjamin Fleury-Steiner has studied homeless African American male veterans of Vietnam, the Persian Gulf, and more recent wars. He found that they had returned to segregated communities collectively traumatized by unemployment, poor and insufficient housing, and widespread racism in criminal justice and other institutions. Unable to find steady work and maintain a stable family life, the men fell into homelessness and became entangled in the criminal justice system. VA programs were experienced as remote and inaccessible (Fleury-Steiner 2012).

Even middle class returnees such as expatriates like Alessi face obstacles to survival when they are in between contracts or become unable to work abroad for one reason or another. Expatriates are often hired by NGOs on one year contracts, and when the year is up and the contract is not renewed, a period of weeks or months may ensue before they can get a contract with another agency. Alessi told me that it is not easy or affordable to get medical insurance or to re-establish credit when he returns to the U.S. Expatriates may not be able to collect Social Security when they are older if they have not paid enough into the system. Alessi often relies on the generosity of his network of friends when he is in the U.S., for a place to stay, dental care on a sliding scale, loan of a vehicle, and help with other issues.

Health care is a survival issue faced by many returnees and it deserves special mention. The reader may think of "food, clothing and shelter" as priorities, but for returnees from war zones, disasters, and prisons, injuries and illnesses associated with their extraordinary experiences may be life threatening or at the very least threatening to the quality of their lives. For example, as mentioned above in chapter 3, first responders to the 9/11 terrorist attacks have experienced many health troubles and difficulties getting access to health care. Joe Gardner, the National Guard veteran I interviewed, returned from Afghanistan with a recurring infection, nothing disabling, but it has to be treated. Fortunately he has adequate medical insurance in his current position. Other veterans have not been so fortunate. Advocacy groups and the media have made the American public aware of the problems that injured veterans of Iraq and Afghanistan have had getting timely and quality medical care through the VA system.

Clearly, not every returnee satisfactorily meets this primary challenge of survival. As we have seen in chapter 3, mental breakdowns, a return to prison, a life on the streets, even death, are costs some returnees bear.

THE SECOND CHALLENGE: DAILY LIFE

Ordinary life places distinct obstacles in the way of people who have been living in an extraordinary culture. This is true even if the returnee goes home to the culture from which he departed. But, as we will see, many people do not return home to their region or nation of origin. Instead, they have to learn how to go about recreating an ordinary life for themselves in a culture they have never functioned in. But let us first consider people returning to their native culture.

Some of the things ordinary people take for granted in daily life are huge obstacles for people returning from extraordinary experiences. Anita Schorr told me that while she had been in the concentration camps, she had forgotten how to read, and although she could add and subtract, she had forgotten how to multiply. A friend helped her learn to read again, and taught her basic math. Kwame Cannon, a young African American man, the son of another survivor of the Greensboro attack by the KKK, recounted his return to ordinary life after serving thirteen years in prison in North Carolina. Cannon had been a child at the time the KKK shot at the marchers. When in his teens, under the influence of an older cousin, he committed some burglaries. Represented by an incompetent lawyer, he agreed to a plea bargain entailing two life sentences. According to Bermanzohn, survivors believe this harsh sentencing was probably offered by the local authorities to retaliate against his mother for standing with the other CWP survivors of the KKK attack who were attempting to get justice for the victims of the shootings. After a "Free Kwame" campaign won widespread support, Cannon was finally freed. He said,

I felt like a time traveler, thrust into the future into an unfamiliar society. CDs, VCRs, cordless phones, personal computers, fax machines—they were all unfamiliar to me. I tried to withdraw twenty dollars from my checking account through an ATM machine. I was struggling to get the machine to accept my card. Willena (his mother) comes over and says, "Here, let me see your ATM card." I handed her my card. She smiled and said, "Kwame, this is your driver's license!" (Bermanzohn 2003:356–57).

Former convicts interviewed by journalist Sabine Heinlein told her they had to remember when at restaurants not to take the silverware with them on their way out—in prison they had the procedure of dropping their utensils in a bucket by the exit. On a less mundane level, one former prisoner told Heinlein he "jerked" when his new girlfriend "touched him without warning." Touching in prison is a sign of provocation and disrespect (Heinlein 2013:161–62).

Some exonerated death row inmates interviewed by Westervelt and Cook developed a habit of "living in the present" because their incarceration and death sentence gave them little or no control over plans for the future. Once released, it was hard to learn how to plan ahead. Some stated that they didn't even try, they just accepted living day to day (Westervelt and Cook 2012:158). Exonerated death row inmates told Westervelt and Cook that one of the biggest needs they had was for what one interviewee called a "decompression" period in which they could "readjust to the daily routines of life—socializing, driving, grocery shopping, learning new technologies—free from the worries of finding a job, paying bills, or finding a permanent home" (Westervelt and Cook 2012:210). Unfortunately, halfway houses or other such supportive housing do not exist for many such former prisoners, and they must adjust to everyday life while facing major problems with the survival issues.

Returnees from extraordinary experiences often describe themselves as irritated by the way people in ordinary life do not take things seriously enough, or the reverse, by the way they "sweat the small stuff" too much. Having faced death, or being challenged to one's limits, physically and emotionally, returnees feel a certain distance from the seemingly petty concerns of others, a distance that usually needs to be kept under wraps, in order to avoid conflict. Cameron Smith, the Army veteran I interviewed, recalled what it was like being in college classrooms with younger students who had gone straight from high school to college. He was dismayed at seeing them texting on their cell phones in class and not even listening to the professors. Lukacs, the child Holocaust survivor, described concealing her annoyance at friends who got upset about the absence of sugar packets on the table at a restaurant where they were having lunch. Joe Gardner, the National Guard veteran, told me "you develop a sense of hate over there," hate for the Taliban and Al Qaeda. When he got back to the U.S. he was surprised at how much hate and anger he felt toward "lazy" and "complaining" American civilians who are "ungrateful" for what they have in the U.S. He said he felt he was not prejudiced before he was deployed to the war zone, but when he returned, he could see himself developing prejudices. He feels his anger stops him from having compassion towards "loafers on welfare with six kids who see movies all day on TV." He resents gangbangers, star musicians, and athletes who want higher salaries when they are already making millions.

Interaction with people in ordinary environments may be challenging in many unexpected or surprising ways. Anita Schorr described to me that she found it very difficult to go to funerals. The first time she went to one, she felt "crazy"—that so much attention was being put on one person who had died, when "millions had been thrown away like garbage." Some white civil rights workers who left the Movement after the rise of Black Power and returned to white communities found it difficult to smoothly interact with whites because they no longer accepted the taken-for-granted assumptions about white superiority (Curry et al. 2000). Denis Goldberg, a leader in the African National Congress in South Africa, was released from prison after many years, and went to London and other places outside South Africa as part of his work for change. Goldberg reported that "when you come out of prison after 22 years, to be in a crowd of people is exhausting . . . after a few hours I said I couldn't take it anymore. I needed to be taken home, meaning prison, because I needed to get out of the noise, and the lights, and the movement all around" (Goldberg 2005: 29).

A former prisoner told Heinlein about his trouble adjusting to riding in the subway again. He felt "disrespected" when people stared at him. "In prison there was no reason to stare unless you wanted to start a fight. The same was true for physical contact. If safety mattered to you, you simply didn't bump into others. In prison you automatically made space for people approaching you, but in the subway there never seemed to be enough space." He also told Heinlein that it took him a while to realize he didn't have to continue to eat the kind of food he used to buy in the prison store—tuna, peanut butter and jelly, calamari—and to figure out what alternative foods to eat (Heinlein 2013:41, 71). Another prisoner, released when he was in his seventies, told Heinlein that his old age was a surprise to him upon release. In prison, no one celebrated birthdays and "time stood still." He had not felt old in prison. Now that he was out, he felt that "it's over for me." He believed he could hardly begin a new life like younger former prisoners, since he was likely to live only another ten years, twenty if he is lucky (Heinlein 2013:164).

One activist in the 1960s New Left movement who had become accustomed to highly politicized relationships with others, as well as secrecy about his activities, was surprised by people's utter disinterest in his background when he returned to a more ordinary life. Mark Rudd was a leader in the student movement in the 1960s and one of the founders of the Weatherman faction of Students for a Democratic Society. He went underground for years after he became wanted by the FBI for several non-lethal bombings. During that time he more or less stopped participating in the extraordinary activities he had been engaged in with the Weatherman group and resumed a more ordinary life. Rudd, with his wife, moved from place to place around the country, never feeling completely safe despite assumed names and various disguises to appearance. But when interacting with ordinary people, Rudd was puzzled by the lack of curiosity about the couple:

> No one ever asked us where we came from, or why, or directly questioned the vague cover story we offered: We're from San Francisco, tired of city life, exploring the West. At first, surprised about this lack of curiosity, I chalked it up to the unique tolerance of Santa Fe, which has seen generations of artists and other outcasts from straight America. But after living as a fugitive for years in other parts of the country, I realized that there is a national characteristic of not inquiring about people's pasts. Perhaps it's possibly due to politeness, or possibly just lack of interest (Rudd 2009:242).

Mark Alessi, the aid worker, had similar experiences with Americans lacking curiosity about his work and life overseas. He said some of his friends say "Hi, I don't know what you really do there, how about going to a ball game?" He is rarely asked about the details of what he does in Africa or Asia. When people ask about his work, they ask in such an offhand way it seems clear to him that they don't want him to fully explain it.

It is impressive to see how Holocaust survivors met the added challenges of being immigrants to countries far from their homelands. Both of the child Holocaust survivors I interviewed had left Europe within a few years of the end of the war. Anita Schorr had taken part in a Zionist camp for youth, and was inspired to immigrate to Israel, where she married and lived on a kibbutz. Highly engaged in the Zionist cause, she went through military training and plunged into work on the kibbutz with enthusiasm. She and her husband left only because they had gotten into an unexpected conflict with kibbutz leaders over some unfair treatment. They got an immigration visa to the United States, where her husband's mother was living with a younger brother. "It's overwhelming to be an immigrant unless you're really rich," said Schorr, "everything is different." Schorr was also disappointed at the low status of women in the United States as compared to Israel. As mentioned earlier, she arrived in the U.S. in 1959, just at the time after World War II when women were being urged to stay at home, raise children, and tend to domestic chores, while the men returning from the war replaced them in jobs and careers. It was a strange experience for a woman who had prioritized having a career, and had gone through military training so that she could, if necessary, defend the Jewish homeland from attack.

Eva Lukacs, like Anita Schorr, went to another country before she came to the U.S. She left her country at the age of sixteen, when a revolution against the Soviet Union was crushed and she felt that things would never change there. Her parents did not want to leave, as she had a brother who was sick, but her fourteen-year-old sister agreed to leave with her and the parents came up with money to pay a peasant who guided people across the border. They made three attempts to cross the border into a non-Communist country. The first time they were intercepted by Russian tanks and the second by her country's army; the third time they were successful. Lukacs went to Vienna, which as a capitalist city seemed so different from the Communist cities. It "seemed gorgeous because of the lights, the goods in the stores, cafes all over." Lukacs had two sets of underwear, one dress, and a pair of heels, plus what she was wearing. In her home country, she had been elegantly dressed, but she felt out of place in Vienna. Later, she emigrated to the United States, and once there, she started school. Because she spoke no English, she was classified as an "imbecile" on a placement test. After learning English, she could speak with Americans but found certain customs puzzling. People would say, "how are you?" but they didn't wait to find out your answer. People would ask her to lunch, but then not follow up. Eventually she adjusted.

Not every returnee manages or even wants to adjust to all the circumstances of everyday life in the ordinary world. Mark Alessi described to me his acute discomfort when he visits home in the U.S. He finds it hard to interact with Americans who are unaware and ungrateful about the economic privileges they enjoy. He described as "otherworldly" TV programs like *Survivor* or *Dancing with the Stars* that American friends and family members try to introduce him to. He said, "I have to leave the room," when *Survivor* comes on. He feels that the media profit by selling Americans fake transformational experiences they enjoy vicariously, without really being affected by the experiences. Alessi is also uncomfortable with how Americans see their country. He believes that Americans see themselves as exporting democracy, yet they treat the sick and the poor and the Muslim population badly, and do not jail the people whose manipulation of the economy resulted in recession. Americans don't know much about the rest of the world, or have much empathy for perspectives of people outside America. They think they live in a happy utopia, and don't realize that people elsewhere can be happier. Alessi looks at America's decaying infrastructure and joblessness and wonders why citizens do not protest more than they do. When he is in the U.S., he prefers to return to Africa or Asia as quickly as possible.

THE THIRD CHALLENGE: RECONSTRUCTION OF SELF AND IDENTITY

"Who am I?" As we saw in part I of the book, an extraordinary experience tends to draw a line through a person's life, such that this question would have been answered one way before the extraordinary experience, and another way after. It is impossible to go back to being the person one was before the experience. Yet, going forward without making some changes is equally impossible, since the self and identity that developed in the extraordinary culture may not quite fit into the ordinary world. A person needs to literally create a new self and new identity.

An important aspect of reconstruction of identity is simply to begin to play an active part in constructing one's roles in society and one's personal qualities. For example, while Anita Schorr took care of her material needs and need for safety, her thoughts turned to becoming a student again so she could develop her knowledge and skills. She wanted to finish her education but there were no programs in place to help a teen who had been out of school since the sixth grade. She was expected to return to the sixth grade to finish her schooling, but Schorr felt "too old" to tolerate being with the younger children. Soon, through determination and perseverance, she managed to get a scholarship to go to an art school, and after a year even found a job in which she could utilize her artistic talents, dressing the windows in a tailor shop. Schorr often did not know how she should behave. She actively coped with this by asking herself, what would my parents tell me to do? She describes herself as turning herself into a "super-obedient child," which in fact she had not been. Schorr described nurturing a variety of positive qualities—especially hope, self-confidence, and perseverance—that enabled her to overcome obstacles and move ahead. Subsequently, she recreated herself as an Israeli, a fighter, a soldier, a commercial artist in the United States, and a wife and mother.

Another dimension to the challenge of creating a new self and identity is making a choice about how to handle presenting information about the former, extraordinary self to others, especially when others resist hearing about it, or seem uninterested or unable to understand what one is telling them. As mentioned earlier, Helen Ebaugh emphasized in *Becoming an Ex* (1988) that many people who leave one identity for another work to incorporate the previous identity into the new one, creating an "ex" identity. In her research, Ebaugh found that others were often greatly curious about the past lives of people with an "ex" identity (Ebaugh 1988:160). However, I have found that in many sorts of extraordinary experiences others seemingly ignore that the experiences happened, or urge forgetfulness or secrecy about the experiences. For example, Charlotte Delbo wrote of her experiences in the French Resistance, including her time in a concentration camp, as "useless knowledge" (Delbo 1995). Murray Polner interviewed an American soldier who had returned from Vietnam, profoundly affected by his service. He went back to his hometown, lived with his parents, went to college, and began to go out to socialize with other young people. He met a girl he had known before the war. "She acted as if she had seen me the night before. It was the same with everyone else. 'You're back huh, what else is new?' It was an effort for me to merely finish the semester." He was most able to have an "ex" identity when he was socializing with other veterans with whom he could express his pride at having served in the Marines, and be open about his reactions to Vietnam (1971:13). In *Fatelessness,* Imre Kertesz's semi-autobiographical memoir of the Holocaust, the central character, Georg, had been sent to Auschwitz at the age of 14. Returning to Budapest after the war, he found his aunt and two uncles, from whom he learns that his father died in a concentration camp and that his mother is alive but has remarried. Visiting with the aunt and uncles, one uncle declared "'before all else . . . you must put the horrors behind you.' Increasingly amazed, I asked, 'Why should I?' 'In order,' he replied, 'to be able to live . . . one cannot start a new life under such a burden,' and I had to admit he did have a point. Except I didn't quite understand how they could wish for something that was impossible." Georg tries in vain to explain to them that he believes that we all take steps to live our own fates:

> I too had lived through a given fate. It had not been my own fate, but I had lived through it, and I simply couldn't understand why they couldn't get it into their heads that I now needed to start doing something with that fate, needed to connect it to somewhere or something; after all, I could no longer be satisfied with the notion that it had all been a mistake, blind fortune, some kind of blunder, let alone that it had not happened.

Georg wants to move on with his life yet refuses to deny that he was an active participant in living his extraordinary experiences in the way he did (Kertesz 2004:256, 259).

Sometimes the absence of an "ex" identity is as much self-imposed as imposed from the outside. As mentioned above, Sally Bermanzohn did not want to speak of her experiences with the CWP for many years due to the repression its members had faced. The child Holocaust survivors, Anita Schorr and Eva Lukacs, both told me that for years they did not talk to anyone about their experiences. Lukacs and her husband, who was also a survivor, promised one another that they would never talk to their children about the Holocaust. They wanted them to have a "normal" childhood. But Lukacs kept the memories in her head, because she felt that if she forgot, then no one else would ever know about what happened. It was a big burden to remember in this way. Schorr told me that she was able to talk to people about her time at the kibbutz, but on the subject of Auschwitz, she was "totally closed." She did not want other people to pity her. She wanted to think of herself as a survivor. Both women avoided presenting themselves to others as Holocaust victims. Eventually, when a university began a project to take oral histories of survivors, they participated, and through that project, child Holocaust survivors began to find one another and talk. Subsequently, both women began to publicly speak of their histories. Lukacs told me that as a result, "the burden in my head was lighter, although not fully alleviated." I will say more about this sort of silence in the next chapter.

The effect on the self of being unable or unwilling to present the "ex" aspect of oneself is to live as a kind of "false self." The idea of a false self is that a person has become split between the self that is known to oneself and the inauthentic presentation of self to others. It is stressful and painful. There is a large amount of "emotions management" involved when presenting a false self (Hochschild 1983).

Another dimension of reconstruction of self and identity relates to survivors of trauma. Survivors of trauma doing the work of self-reconstruction may need to mourn the loss of the innocent, pre-traumatized self that is gone forever (Herman 1992:189). Mourning, according to Herman, is not the same as forgiveness or reconciliation. Forgiveness depends on having identifiable perpetrators who are willing to admit guilt and ask for forgiveness. If one's torturers are not willing or available to do this, then perhaps the only option is to mourn and then go on. One mourns the loss of a self the way one would mourn the loss of a loved other. I cannot say with certainty whether Schorr went through a mourning process but some things she told me lead me to suspect that she did. She told me that she had lifelong regrets about not getting a formal education. Although she went to art school, had other educational experiences, and a successful career as a commercial artist, she felt she lacked the "overview" that a person gets through formal schooling. Lukacs similarly expressed some regrets that she had not known enough about American ways to apply for scholarships when she was ready to go to college. Although she had a successful career as a teacher and marketing consultant, she seemed to also be wondering what she had missed. She had been an excellent student and would probably have been able to get into any college, but due to lack of funds, she enrolled in a public college where tuition was low. It was a good college, but did not have the same prestige and afford the same opportunities as another college might have.

People who have endured slavery, especially those enslaved for prostitution, seem to have a particularly difficult time restoring the self and identity in the ordinary world. A book edited by Kevin Bales and Zoe Trodd, *To Plead Our Own Cause: Personal Stories by Today's Slaves* (2008) contains poignant stories of people who have been freed from slavery. Inez, who was trafficked in 1997 from Mexico to the U.S. for sexual slavery, suffered brutal and degrading treatment at a place of prostitution in Florida. A year after being freed, she stated, "I cannot seem to get past the ordeal . . . I lack

confidence and never feel secure . . . I am trying hard to be the person I was
before I came to the United States." Another woman, Rosa, trafficked from
Mexico to Florida when she was only fourteen, said "I cannot forget what has
happened. I can't put it behind me. I find it nearly impossible to trust people.
I still feel shame" (Bales and Trodd 2008:184, 187).

When returnees have been *engulfed* by the extraordinary culture, as discussed in chapter 2, the task of reconstructing identity is especially difficult,
and can be lengthy. Karen Armstrong, a British ex-nun, has written two
memoirs, the first about her life in the convent, the second about her struggle
to reconstruct her identity after leaving (Armstrong [1981]2005; Armstrong
2004). She had entered the convent in 1962 at the age of seventeen. This was
before the Church had begun to liberalize life in its orders, and convent life
was very rigid and confining. She had been drawn by a passionate interest in
the religious life, the desire "to know God," yet found herself unable to live
within the strictures of the convent. She left after seven years, but then found
it difficult to undo the habits of thought and feeling she had learned there. In
a visit back to the convent to see a former colleague, Armstrong spoke with
one of the nuns in leadership. She told the Reverend Mother about some
physical symptoms she was having and attributed them to her difficulties in
adjusting to life outside: "I trained to be a nun for five solid years . . . it's a
training that shapes you at a very deep level. And I just can't *stop* being a
nun. I need a new training—one that is equally intensive—to turn me into a
secular" (Armstrong 2004:69). Armstrong's quest to reconstruct her identity
took decades; her journey will be discussed further in the next chapter.

Returnees who are stigmatized and repressed by society based on their
experiences have special struggles with how they are going to see their
extraordinary identity. They have to decide whether they will accept society's condemnation of their extraordinary experience, or somehow struggle
against the negative characterization of it. Sociologists who study deviant
populations—such as juvenile delinquents, prisoners, or the homeless—have
found that having a stigmatized master status can reinforce *engulfment* or
contribute to its emergence (Snow and Anderson 1993; Schur 1971). According to Michelle Alexander, young African Americans—many of whom have
become entangled in the criminal justice system—may strike out against
stigmas against them, even in ways that may be self-defeating, such as embracing a "gangsta culture." They choose to embrace the stigma and turn it
around on the stigmatizers. According to Alexander,

> it is helpful to step back and put the behavior of young black men who appear
> to embrace "gangsta culture" in the proper perspective. There is absolutely
> nothing abnormal or surprising about a severely stigmatized group embracing
> their stigma. Psychologists have long observed that when people feel hopeless-
> ly stigmatized, a powerful coping strategy—and often the only apparent route

to self-esteem—is embracing one's stigmatized identity. Hence, "black is beautiful" and "gay pride"—slogans and anthems of political movements aimed at ending not only legal discrimination but the stigma that justified it. For stigmatized Black youth, "embracing the stigma of criminality is an act of rebellion—an attempt to carve out a positive identity in a society that offers them little more than scorn, contempt, and constant surveillance . . . The problem, of course, is that embracing criminality—while a natural response to the stigma—is inherently self-defeating and destructive . . . Black crime cripples the black community and does no favors to the individual offender" (Alexander 2012:170–172).

Death row exonerees face a somewhat different situation. As discussed in chapter 3, they often return to communities in which public officials and many citizens still do not accept their innocence despite exoneration. They are stigmatized as ex-cons, yet they know they have committed no crime. They reject engulfment by the prison culture and engage in a struggle to convince others of their innocence. This struggle becomes a central aspect of their reconstruction of identity (Westervelt and Cook 2012:174–75, 188–89).

Finally, the reconstruction of self and identity is not a short term or simple process; some people go through a series of false starts, or flounder around, as they begin, especially if they are still trying to deal with the other challenges, such as material survival, or if they are mourning the loss of the person they were before a traumatic experience. Nando Parrado's description of the period of his life immediately after returning from the disaster in the Andes can be seen in this light. He had become somewhat of a celebrity, which enabled him to party with beautiful women. He later realized that carousing was helping him to fill up a numbness he felt at the time. He then turned to racing sports cars, and spent two years racing motorcycles and stock cars around the world. It was an exciting life, but eventually he met a woman and fell in love, and realized that he could not have a life with her if he kept on traveling around the world racing cars. They married, and he went into his father's business, which he found very satisfying, and later found a second career working with his wife to produce and host several programs on Uruguayan television about travel, nature, current events, and fashion. He and his wife also had two children and devoted themselves to them (Parrado 2006:249–58).

Like the challenges of survival and returning to daily life, the challenge of reconstructing the self and identity is one that not everyone meets successfully. Cohen, in *The Victims Return,* wrote about survivors of the *Gulag* who did not manage to go forward after being released. They were so frightened of being rearrested that it was almost as if they were still imprisoned. Even a great memoirist, Varlam Shalamov, was characterized by a contemporary as seemingly "frozen by his experience . . . like a blackened tree struck by lightning which will never again become green" (2012:58). Charlotte Delbo,

the World War II French resister, pointed out that trauma survivors seem
unable to construct a fully new self in the present when they cannot get what
she called a "second skin" of intrusive traumatic memories to become like
normal memories (Langer 1995:xi). A film, *Plenty,* based on a play by David
Hare, won favorable reviews for its portrayal of a character who became
stuck in an extraordinary experience and was unable to move on afterward
(Papp and Pressman 1985). The central character is Susan Traherne, an English woman who has taken part in the French resistance behind enemy lines
in France. While there, she has a brief romance with a British agent who has
parachuted down to connect with the Resistance. When she returns to England after the war, she finds ordinary life boring and trivial, in comparison
with the romance and excitement of her years in the Resistance. "A woman
who once lived intensely, and now feels that she is hardly living at all," she
treats her husband and others around her with disrespect and leads a disturbed life (Ebert 1985).

THE FOURTH CHALLENGE: REINTERPRETING THE MEANING
OF THE EXTRAORDINARY EXPERIENCE

As discussed in chapter 2, the meaning or purpose of one's life is an important part of identity, and people going through extraordinary experiences may
have an interpretation of the purpose of their lives that is rooted in the
importance of the extraordinary experience (e.g., defeating an enemy,
achieving freedom, or serving God). After return to the ordinary world, an
individual's perspective on the meaning of the extraordinary experience is
likely to be shaken. This is because they will be exposed to new experiences
and education and will have interactions with others in the ordinary world
who at the very least may not see the extraordinary experience the same way,
and at worst, may see it as morally wrong or shameful. If nothing else, the
principle of *cognitive dissonance* in psychology will create pressure towards
a changed perspective: when new perceptions contradict existing ideas, the
mind works tirelessly to try to make new sense of the situation.

Combat veterans may struggle with their moral beliefs in regard to being
in combat and killing (Sherman: 2011, 2015). This was true of two of the
veterans I interviewed. Andres Beaumont, the young Marine, had gone on to
college after leaving the military, and studied history and political science.
He said he feels bad for enemy fighters who died, but has no regret or
remorse. He told me that when he faced having to shoot to kill an enemy
soldier in Afghanistan, a soldier who was preparing to kill him, "it was
understood, when we went in, both of us" that this could happen. He feels
okay with the idea that he was trained to kill and fired on enemy soldiers
when he had to, to save his fellow soldiers. He described soldiers like him-

self, however, as having an "inner judging" process going on in the mind. He told me that he thought the mind has a "constant courtroom, or a judge." He felt that in his own case, this was currently minimized like a small computer window, and no one else would know it was going on. But he said he didn't know if he would always feel this way. He thought it might be possible that when he gets older and closer to the end of his natural life, he might begin to wonder, "Is it a sin, what I did?" According to Beaumont, the moral commandment, "Thou shalt not kill," does not put a condition on killing. Joe Gardner, the National Guard veteran, also thought about the morality of what he had done in combat, but was less troubled. He said that he would advise other returnees, "don't over-justify" what you did. "If it was wrong, think you did what you had to, to protect your friends or your country . . . if your command doesn't think it was wrong, it probably wasn't."

Mark Rudd, the 1960s student leader mentioned above, had embraced the Weatherman organization's philosophy of armed struggle. The group believed that sooner or later the masses of working class Americans would develop a "revolutionary consciousness" when actions by revolutionaries would make them aware of the destructive nature of the capitalist system. The group had also completely rejected mainstream values about personal life, from monogamy to mind-altering drugs to standards of health and cleanliness. The Weatherman members became more and more isolated from the rest of the 1960s movements, and unable to achieve their revolutionary dreams. As described in Rudd's memoir, *Underground,* he had doubts about what the group was doing, but he was so caught up in the culture of the group and its way of thinking, that he was unable to detach himself. Rudd finally left the organization in 1977, depressed, and by then a fugitive from the law wanted on various criminal charges in connection with the student revolt at Columbia University in 1968 and Weatherman struggles with the police in Chicago in 1970. After he and his wife had spent years underground, they decided to surface; Rudd managed to get his charges reduced to misdemeanors and was sentenced to two years' probation and a $2,000 fine. Subsequently, he had various experiences that transformed his thoughts about the use of violence for social change. He visited the New York City office of the War Resisters League, a pacifist organization begun after World War I that is against all forms of violence. "They treated me with human decency and seemed to understand the conflicts I had lived with during all the years underground. I found that I could talk with them, about both my history and their nonviolent ideas. In time I would join the WRL and take their pledge 'not to support any kind of war'" (Rudd 2009:299). He became a college teacher at a community college in New Mexico, where he was in touch with over a hundred students each semester from working class backgrounds and learned how they really thought about the system in comparison with the Weatherman fantasies. For years Rudd felt guilt and shame for his part in building a movement that he had come to see as destructive of itself and the larger student movement. After 2003, his interpretation of his extraordinary experiences shifted again, due to new experiences. A documentary film, *The Weather Underground,* was made about the group. Rudd was featured in the film, both as a kid of twenty and in the present, and he became involved in speaking tours to many schools and colleges in association with showings of the film. "In conversations with young people since 2003, I've found that Weatherman's failures are less important to them than the simple astonishing fact that we existed." When Rudd found that young people of today see the relevance of the 1960s youth movement to their own lives now, during this time of globalization and war, he became inspired to "rediscover a voice that I bottled up for two and a half decades . . . (and to reclaim) what I can be proud of: Along with millions of other people, I was part of a movement of history—that's what a 'movement' is, after all, a shift of history caused by millions—that helped end the war in Vietnam. Combined with the civil rights movement, the period was American democracy's finest hour." Rudd hopes that telling his story will help young people "figure out what they can do to build a more just and peaceful world. At the very least, it might show them some pitfalls to avoid" (2009:ix, x, 299, 303).

Survivors of the *Gulag* in the Soviet Union who began to return beginning in the 1940s and 1950s had to decide whether they would identify with the Communist Party's point of view, and look back on their arrest and imprisonment as somehow justified, or whether they would see themselves as the survivors of an unjust and repressive regime. As mentioned in chapter 3, many *Gulag* survivors actually sought to re-join or join the Party upon their release, even though it often took many years of persistent effort to achieve this aim. Many of them had identified with the Party and the cause of building Socialism before their arrest and could not bear the thought of life outside the Party. One survivor explained that he "found solace in his belief in the truth of the Party" while he was confined. He had spent nearly twenty years first in an Arctic camp, and then in exile, yet he said that he dreamed of re-joining the Party. Some released in the Khrushchev years believed that Khrushchev was trying to lead the Party back to Leninist values that Stalin had forsaken. A writer, Galina Serebryakova, who spent twenty-one years in the *Gulag,* proclaimed that the "main tragedy" for the victims was not torture or being separated from their children, but the "fate of the proletarian revolution, the fate of the Party." Even children of *Gulag* survivors joined the Party in order to support Khrushchev and in the hope that their parents' lives would be redeemed (Adler 2004:29, Cohen 2012:64–65). For others returning from the *Gulag*, the motive to be a Party member was connected with their struggle for material survival. Being a Party member made it easier to get a job. A rare few *Gulag* returnees actually achieved successful careers in the Soviet system, becoming leaders in the military, science, prominent actors, sports stars, and the like. On the other hand, many others spoke out against the system. Such people contributed directly or indirectly to the dissident movements that would eventually support the dismantling of the Soviet Union and struggle to build democracy in Russia and the other nations that emerged from the Soviet Union's collapse. Cohen, in *The Victims Return,* describes "professional zeks," who wore "their camp experience like a badge of honor." Memoirs and fictional works about the *Gulag,* as well as works of art, raised awareness about the injustices that had happened under Stalin. In the conservative years after Krushchev, returnees played an important role in the uncensored manuscripts called *samizdat,* which criticized the system, reminding the Soviet population of the crimes of Stalin and calling for democratic reforms. They founded organizations such as the Memorial Society that sought for and uncovered mass graves, and Return, which published survivor memoirs. In the years after Khrushchev when the Party once again became more repressive, some of the *zeks* who had returned to the Party renounced it (Cohen 2012:58–60, 63, 85, 105, 139, 141, 144, 169).

Mark Rudd, and many of the *Gulag* survivors, distanced themselves from many aspects of their extraordinary experiences as they reconstructed their identities. In contrast, others have drawn great and poignant meaning from their extraordinary experiences, seeing their ordinary lives in completely new ways upon return. Prisoners have found great meaning in their experiences. For example, some experience a religious conversion in prison. A study of 75 inmates who had converted to Christianity while in prison discovered that they felt redeemed of their crimes and that they now had a life purpose, both in prison and upon release, to proselytize for their faith (Maruna and Wilson et al. 2006). As mentioned in chapter 2, Nando Parrado described in *Miracle in the Andes* a great transformation in his thinking about himself and the entire meaning of life. The brush with death gave him the insight that life was about love, and he began living in the light of this awareness (Parrado 2006:261). "This is the simple wisdom that will always light my life: I have loved, passionately, fearlessly, with all my heart and all my soul, and I have been loved in return. For me, this is enough." He described himself as living a life full of gratitude at the love he can give and receive, and at the simple joys of ordinary days (Parrado 2006:264).

Linda Nelson, the former nun I interviewed, had been deeply committed to the Catholic views she had learned at the convent. After leaving, she continued as a practicing Catholic, attending services and becoming a leader in various church activities. But she also became very aware of contradictions between her beliefs and the realities of local churches. For example, she was deeply disturbed by clergy abuse of children. She struggled with this and other issues, and eventually left the Catholic Church to participate in a Protestant congregation and to develop her own individual sense of spirituality.

Some returnees do not fully recognize a positive meaning in their extraordinary experience until years later. Sally and Paul Bermanzohn each left the Communist Workers Party in the 1980s when they became critical of a lack of democracy within the Party. For years, Paul still believed that capitalism needed to go, and be replaced with a more just and equal system. He also believed that a revolutionary party was needed to make this happen. But Paul was no longer politically involved. He was absorbed in his work—he had become the director of a psychiatric day center—and his family life. This did not make him feel very good about himself. "Over the years, I kind of marinated in that disgust with myself at my apathy." He described himself as "depressed, demoralized." It took a long time for him to separate the positive meaning he found in the organizing work he had done in the South from the negative meaning the CWP had come to have for him. But when he went to North Carolina for a twentieth anniversary commemoration of the KKK attack, he saw some of the former comrades still struggling to bring out the truth about what had happened. This inspired him, and when he returned home he got involved in a local campaign against genetically-engineered foods. His life took a new direction. "I have returned to my calling as a fighter for justice. That's my life." Paul now balances being a doctor with activism in his community, making life more complex, and leaving him little time to rest, but he feels "much more energetic, much more alive" (Bermanzohn 2003:324, 349–50).

Survivors of traumatic experiences may struggle to understand why they survived, while others did not. A survivor whose family, friends, or even entire community have been killed may circle around the questions, "Why me?" "Why did I survive?" over and over unless or until they come up with a satisfactory answer. This quest for meaning has been termed "survivor guilt." The child Holocaust survivors I interviewed, Schorr and Lukacs, described themselves as plagued by these questions for years. Schorr told me that she feels this is one of the biggest challenges survivors face: to find an answer to the question of why you survived, and pursue that answer. Today Schorr speaks to middle school students about her experiences in the Holocaust, when she was the same age they are now. She explains that the Nazis were able to commit the unspeakable cruelties they did because not enough people opposed them. She makes the analogy to bullies in the schools, and urges the children to "be heroes" and stand up when someone is mistreating someone else. She feels that perhaps this is why she survived, so that she can carry this message. But she still isn't always sure if it is "enough of a reason."

Lukacs told me that she was happy to be alive but felt "unworthy of the grace of being alive." She wondered why she survived because "I am nobody, not someone with real talent, like an Einstein." Eventually she realized that maybe she was alive for a purpose, to be the voice of the children who had died. She became involved in doing interviews of survivors for an oral history project, and also made documentary films. She thinks it is important to teach young people to be proud of being Jews, since Hitler wanted to erase Jews from the earth, and she teaches classes at religious schools on the Holocaust and on the history of anti-Semitism. I will return to Lukacs and Schorr's purposes in the next chapter.

THE FIFTH CHALLENGE: DEVELOPING NEW RELATIONSHIPS, RENEWING OLD RELATIONSHIPS

Although some people exiting the extraordinary do so in groups and do not want for company, many exit as individuals and must make their way alone into new relationships. Establishing such relationships goes hand-in-hand with the reconstruction of identity and meaning, since it is the very nature of the self to exist in relation to others. In addition to new relationships, old relationships, such as family and friends, will also need to be recreated. It is impossible for a person greatly transformed to simply fit neatly back into past roles and relationships, even if everyone around them unthinkingly expects this to happen. For survivors of traumatic experiences who learned to distrust and fear other people, and who may be filled with guilt and shame about their experiences, the challenge of establishing relationships may be even greater. As we have seen, they may impose isolation upon themselves, while at the same time, others are hesitant to talk to them about their past. As in the case of the other challenges, meeting the challenge is not a linear process; new relationships may break up, putting a person on a renewed search for lovers or friends, old relationships may die and be reborn later, and so on. Nor do all returnees meet the challenge successfully. Some returnees isolate themselves, or develop only superficial relationships.

Two-thirds of the exonerated death row inmates interviewed by Westervelt and Cook were fortunate to have relationships with family, friends, or lawyers who supported them during their entanglement with the criminal justice system and upon release. One said that his sister "was there for me from the beginning to the end . . . it helped me. Without her, I don't know" (Westervelt and Cook 2012:160). Relationships that were there before, during and after exoneration enabled these people to have a kind of seamless transition that many other returnees from extraordinary experiences do not.

The difficulty of simply fitting back into old roles and relationships is dramatically illustrated by the story of a Vietnam veteran interviewed by Murray Polner. John Durant had been a helicopter pilot in Vietnam, who flew in to pick up dead and wounded soldiers and take them back to hospitals or for grave registration. He saw horrendous carnage of American troops, and witnessed atrocities committed by the South Vietnamese army. Shortly after he had returned home to his hometown, Bangor, Maine, he went for a walk in Orono, a small town next to Bangor.

> The first thing he noticed was the contrast between his town, standing whole and comfortable, and Vietnam . . . his mind kept returning to Vietnamese hovels, to a scene in which a young woman lay in a grass hammock, giving birth, her sense of humor and humanity still intact. The memories and the town overwhelmed him; he looked again at the houses and stillness, and turned away, vomiting.

Durant eventually married, and became active with an antiwar group of veterans. He felt great satisfaction when he would make a presentation critical of the war, and other veterans would come up afterward and tell him they felt the same way (Polner 1971:47, 63).

Another young Vietnam veteran interviewed by Polner spoke of his alienation from older men in his hometown who had eagerly sought out his company. David Chambers held conservative political views and was proud of his service in Vietnam. He returned home to the small town in New Jersey where he had grown up. His father was a proud veteran of the Marines, and had fought in the Pacific in World War II. When Chambers returned home, he went with his father to the American Legion Hall, where his father often hung out with buddies who were veterans of World War II and the Korean War. The talk turned to the war, and the men expressed hawkish views that Chambers agreed with. "Only something bothered me. These men, including my father, had not been there. . . I could listen to them if they had been in Nam, but everybody else was suspect. Their arguments were so pat; they all seemed so damn sure. But I was *there*" (Polner 1971:7). As to civilians who had never served in the military, "No one seemed to care. Life just went on as always, and no one seemed to know a war was on." Eventually Chambers went on to establish himself as a college student; he finished college with a major in business. While in college, he found joy in taking part in a tutoring program for children in the African American community. He continued to interact with his father's buddies at the Legion Hall, and was thinking about running for the post commander position so that he could try to educate the members towards views that were conservative, but less parochial (Polner 1971:10, 17–18).

Some survivors of the *Gulag* in the former Soviet Union faced unique challenges in their relationships. There are many stories of one spouse patiently waiting for the other's return, and of families being happily reunited. But others experienced great difficulties. A child might reject a returning parent, due to the parent's strange appearance and bad moods, or just because the parent seemed so different from the way they had once been. A parent might be afraid to tell a child what they had learned in the *Gulag*, if the child idolized Stalin. Some spouses had been apart for so long and become so different, they could not reunite, even if both of them had been in the *Gulag* (Applebaum 2003:518–19; Cohen 2002:69–73). As mentioned in chapter 3, some spouses had renounced a partner taken away, and/or divorced and remarried. Some people had been sent to camps containing both sexes, found someone new there, and married. Some returnees married other survivors, believing that only another *zek* could understand them.

Karen Armstrong, the British ex-nun, wrote in her second memoir about her return to her family of origin. The convent had discouraged friendship among the nuns, and "the atmosphere was frigid." Her family was a close and affectionate one, but now Armstrong "shied away from any intimacy, could not bear to be touched or embraced, and could speak to my family only in the rather formal, distant way of nuns" (Armstrong 2004:26).

After Joe Gardner returned from Afghanistan, he received a great deal of support from his relationship with his girlfriend. She had been his high school sweetheart, and although they had broken up in the past, they had gotten back together. Joe said that his girlfriend, who has a B.A. in psychology and is now studying for a M.A. degree, "kept me grounded." When he first came back, he could not stand to be in crowds. When he would go to a big party, he would get into a fight. His girlfriend "put a halt" to this behavior. Likewise, he began to drink alcohol to try to put himself to sleep, and "it grew." When his girlfriend complained, he stopped. He also tried to give up a two pack a day cigarette habit.

Not all returnees meet the challenge of establishing relationships, at least not right away. Describing herself after she had recently left the convent, Karen Armstrong wrote, "love was beyond me, even friendship was difficult" (Armstrong 2004:29).

This chapter has explored five challenges faced by returnees. The next chapter turns to the strategies individuals use to deal with the challenges that were the subject of this chapter. It focuses especially on the last three challenges— reconstruction of identity, reinterpretation of the extraordinary experience, and establishing relationships. This is not because material survival or re-learning how to deal with everyday life are not important. They are, but in my research, I found that returnees often identified the last three challenges as the areas where they received the *least* help, so I decided it would be best to shine a spotlight on them.

Chapter Five

Strategies for Returning to the Ordinary World

As I read memoirs and autobiographies, and interviewed returnees, I found that there are some typical strategies that returnees pursue, consciously or unconsciously, as they work to reconstruct their identities, reinterpret their extraordinary experiences, and re-establish relationships with others. In the first part of this chapter I explain what I mean by "strategy" and describe each of the strategies I identified. After that, I evaluate the strategies, presenting my views as to which strategies seem to be most successful, not only in meeting the bottom line of the various challenges, but also in arriving at greater satisfaction or happiness in life.

I hope this chapter will provide some clarification about the consequences of choosing one strategy over another. I want to note here that I do not mean to claim that every returnee consciously chooses and pursues one or more of the strategies discussed in this chapter. Some may be unaware that they have choices, or may have not fully reflected on their options. It occurs to me that in such situations, this chapter could be seen as a kind of checklist of possibilities to be considered.

STRATEGIES

By strategy I mean a plan of action in pursuit of a goal. Strategy can be seen as an aspect or dimension of human agency and the ongoing process of active self-construction that was discussed in chapter 2. Some strategies are more oriented to the interior, that is, they involve people's private thoughts, feelings, and stories (narratives) about the self. Others are more oriented to the outside, that is, they involve how people present themselves to others, the stories (narratives) they tell about themselves to others, and the choices they make about connecting with others. Some strategies involve more "processing" of the extraordinary experience, others require less. By "processing," I mean conscious reflection on one's life as a totality, before, during, and after the extraordinary experiences. Each strategy is an individual choice; however, certain options may be dictated by others—individuals and/or institutions. As we saw in chapter 3, sometimes a person's choices are severely limited by the social context.

I have identified nine strategies used by individuals, and I find it fascinating that they can be seen in operation across recent centuries and around the world. Many of the strategies are, by the way, not mutually exclusive. An individual may pursue more than one simultaneously. The strategies, in brief are: 1) Repression: attempting to forget one's memories of the extraordinary experience and move on as though it had never happened. 2) Silence or secrecy: presenting oneself to others as if the experience had never happened. 3) Nostalgia: living as though one's life were only meaningful during the extraordinary experience. 4) Renewal: seeking to recapture the emotional qualities of the extraordinary experience by pursuing other, different experiences. 5) Therapy: seeking insights and guidance through therapeutic work with trained professionals such as psychiatrists, psychologists, or social workers. 6) Personal healing practices: devising healing activities or rituals of one's own. 7) Support: joining groups with others who lived through the same or similar experiences, to share stories and offer assistance. 8) Political action: telling one's story to the public with the aim of helping other survivors or preventing negative extraordinary experiences from happening again. 9) Recognition of continuity: awareness that there is a continuity in one's self and identity before, during, and after the extraordinary experience.

THE FIRST STRATEGY: REPRESSION

In American lingo, this is the strategy of "just suck it up." Returnees try to forget what happened, and go on with life as though they had never had the extraordinary experience. An example of this is one of the Vietnam veterans interviewed by Murray Polner. Fred Schoenwald was the son of German immigrants. His father and uncle and other relatives had served in the German Army during World War II. Fred had served as a combat medic in Vietnam and had "seen more sustained, intense fighting than any other veteran" Polner interviewed. When Schoenwald returned, his parents were warm and welcoming but seemed reticent to ask him about what he had gone through. Finally, he asked his mother whether she wanted to hear about it, and she said she didn't, explaining:

"We know what war is like . . . You had to go through it because we are only nobodies who have no say. You had to follow orders, just like Papa had to, and everyone else we know. You are alive now, just as we are. That's because we didn't argue and we followed their orders without any fuss." She was very upset—I know my mother and she was upset. "I tell you this, Freddie. Don't think about it anymore. Don't talk about it. Soon it will leave you, like it did us" . . . That was the best advice I ever received in my life. From then on . . . I've blotted everything out. That's the way it always will be. It never happened. It was all a bad dream. I sleep well.

According to Polner, Schoenwald suffered difficulties as a result of his decision to repress his memories. He tried to establish a relationship with a girl he loved, but it foundered because he wanted her to understand what he had been through, and yet he couldn't bring himself to tell her. He attained a B.A. in engineering, and began to study religion in his free time. He refused to stay in touch with the author. Did he sleep quietly? Polner thought probably not (Polner 1971:98–100, 107).

Using alcohol or drugs to "numb" oneself can be associated with repression. As Westervelt and Cook point out in their book on exonerated death row inmates, when someone is suffering from trauma, using alcohol or drugs is a way to "dissociate from the distress, suppress or 'wall off' intrusive thoughts about the event, and dampen the survivor guilt many feel" (Westervelt and Cook 2012:138).

THE SECOND STRATEGY: SILENCE AND SECRECY

Some returnees do not repress their memories of their past, but they deliberately withhold knowledge of their past from others. This may be through silence, or through secrecy. Silence and secrecy are not quite the same thing. Secrecy involves deliberately lying in order to conceal something. Silence involves simply omitting part of one's life story. Either way, the effect is that a person's self-presentation is not authentic or is not complete, which can result in a *false self*, and some degree of emotional turmoil. Silence or secrecy about an extraordinary experience is not unusual. Polner, who interviewed 204 Vietnam veterans, noted that most of the veterans he spoke with preferred that no one knew they had been in Vietnam (Polner 1971:163). Ebaugh found that ex-nuns in the 1970s struggled with whether to reveal their pasts to people, and especially when they began to date, because there were stereotypes about nuns being naive and expectations that ex-nuns would have "certain religious qualities and values" (Ebaugh 1988:160). The former nun I interviewed did not talk to anyone for years about her background; she did not want people to see her as "weird." Silence among Holocaust survivors who emigrated to the U.S. was widespread and had complex causes.

They often felt that no one would believe them, because their experiences were too terrifying. They also had feelings of guilt and shame about what had happened, a desire to not be seen as helpless victims, as well as fears about presenting themselves as different, given the persistent anti-Semitism in the U.S. (Stein 2014: 5–9)

Silence or secrecy may be one way to deal with the challenge of presentation of self; however, it seems to be accompanied by emotional difficulties (Stein 2014: 6). It would seem that silence or secrecy are especially unhelpful when returnees are suffering from PTSD. Each of the two child Holocaust survivors I interviewed spent about twenty years in silence. One told me, when she tried to talk to older survivors, they said "what do you know, you were just a child." And she couldn't talk to Americans either, since Americans were not curious. Both survivors had nightmares, and, as mentioned earlier, Schorr's went on for around twenty years.

Shelly Bermanzohn, who survived the KKK attack on the march in North Carolina, says in her memoir that she was unable to talk about her experiences for many years. She went to graduate school in urban planning, and became highly engaged with her studies and the other students. Yet 5 semesters later, with her M.A. in hand, she had never spoken to anyone about her extraordinary experiences. She said that she felt like "a homosexual who was in the closet, hiding a major part of my life . . . Underneath, I felt deep pain, even if nobody could see it." In contrast, her husband Paul, was unable to present himself without in some way explaining what had happened. He had a limp, and paralysis in one arm, visible signs of his experiences. Shelly Bermanzohn went on to a Ph.D. program in political science and resolved to "come out" for her own "psychological stability" (Bermanzohn 2003:337–38).

Sometimes silence or secrecy is pursued due to stigmatization of the extraordinary experience. This point was introduced in chapter 3 in discussing the situation of returning *Gulag* survivors and American prisoners. Silence due to stigmatization is also pursued by exonerated death row inmates. Westervelt and Cook found that some exonerees preferred to tell people about their history only after the person had gotten a chance to know them as persons without a stigma ("selective disclosure") (Westervelt and Cook 2012:188). One inmate moved to a new community where no one knew him, carrying selective disclosure to an extreme. "This puts innocence at the core of his identity by almost erasing any evidence that it was ever in question" (Westervelt and Cook 2012:191). Such an extreme of silence borders on repression and one wonders whether this exoneree sometimes struggles emotionally with the gap between his two realities.

Another type of stigmatization comes from the country of Colombia, which has been in the throes of civil conflicts and drug wars for many years. In recent times, combatants have been encouraged to return to an ordinary life. Among the returnees are people involved on all sides of the conflicts: members of the paramilitary, or death squads, that backed the government, and members of revolutionary organizations that were against the government. One researcher interviewed ex-combatants to find out why they left the paramilitary and what their process of return has been like. She found that many concealed their pasts due to a stigma that exists against former combatants. People think they cannot be trusted because they were once killers. One respondent told her about another ex-combatant who had been fired from a job as soon as the employers discovered his past. In addition to stigmas, there was also the possibility of retaliation by the group that was left behind (Barrios n.d.:18–20).

A similar situation has been reported for people who participated in guerrilla armies during the movement against apartheid in South Africa. Laura Heideman interviewed former soldiers from two anti-apartheid armies for her M.A. thesis at the University of Wisconsin, Madison. When apartheid was overcome, these soldiers were demobilized and returned home. Despite government programs to help with reintegration, they faced stigmas from members of society, who feared them as having been terrorists. Many therefore concealed their pasts in applying for jobs, only to lose the jobs later when employers found out. According to Heideman, some of this was due to racism in white-owned firms, but not all stigmatization could be connected to racism (Heideman 2006).

Silence and the stigmas against disabled people are highlighted in Ron Kovic's book, *Born on the Fourth of July* (1976). Kovic's story was told in part in chapter 1. Paralyzed from the waist down in a firefight, when Kovic returned to a hospital in the U.S. to heal, he decided to be silent with his family about his anger and bitterness over his condition: "I hide all that from them and talk about the other, more pleasant things, the things they want to hear" (1976:26–27).

THE THIRD STRATEGY: NOSTALGIA

Nando Parrado's father admonished him: "The sun will come up tomorrow and the day after that, and the day after that. Don't let this be the most important thing that ever happens to you" (Parrado 2006: 245–46). That is exactly what some returnees do. To some returnees, the extraordinary experience was so profoundly important, exciting, or meaningful that nothing else in life quite compares, and the returnee goes through life never totally engaged, always a bit detached, always comparing the pale present to the colorful past. Vivian Gornick, in *The Romance of American Communism,* writes of former members of the American Communist Party who could not bring themselves to participate in any other sort of politics. She interviewed Jerome Rindzer, an Arizona surgeon, whose life was filled with dedication to the practice of medicine, and who felt an obligation to his profession. But to Rindzer, in the past, politics had been everything, and politics meant an exhilarating connection among ideology, and party, and political action. Once he had left the Communist Party, he looked around at other activist possibilities that were emerging. But he was critical of the movements of the 1960s because of their lack of structure and ideology. "The years when I was a Communist, bar none, were the best years of my life. The relation for me between the personal and the historical was intense, deeply felt, fully realized. Now, I live an entirely personal life, removed from the larger world. I feel no interest in anything beyond my work . . . I've made peace with my life, but I have no illusions that I live a life of larger meaning" (Gornick 1977:195).

Could this be related to the way that the brain structures memory? As discussed in chapter 2, *traumatic* memories persist because they are deeply etched into the brain. Could this also be true of memories of especially *positive* experiences? Gornick summarized several cases similar to the doctor's, and hypothesized that what they know (rationally) about the Party's authoritarianism does not lead them to an identity with a new set of politics, because they are "guided by an emotional frame of reference that cannot be wrenched from the socket of an old and passionate experience inextricably bound up with disciplined structure" (Gornick 1977:202). I spoke with a therapist who is a highly skilled practitioner of EMDR, a type of therapy for PTSD (see below, under "The Fifth Strategy: Psychotherapy"). She explained that people with positive memories like Rindzer's often have thoughts attached to the memories like "I can't let go" or "Life is meaningless now" attached to them. If the memory can be reprocessed so that one remembers it as positive, but *over*, in the past, *done,* then a person may be able to focus on their current life and love it more. She commented that this type of "frozen grief" is not discussed much in the literature on trauma, but is something that trauma therapists often see (Payson 2012).

Some civil rights workers have expressed nostalgia about their experiences. For example, Barbara Jones Omolade had gone from New York City to work in the Atlanta SNCC office because as a young African American woman, she wanted to work for freedom. She wrote later that "for nearly twenty years I continued to search for and attempted to recreate the 'beloved community' of SNCC." She became unable to find it and described herself as continuing "the political mission of SNCC, albeit without its sense of community" (Omolade 2012:388–89, 393–94). Another SNCC worker, Helen O'Neal-McCray, an African American woman who was involved in the movement in Mississippi wrote later, "When I think of SNCC and the Mississippi Movement, it is as if I watched a great drama unfolding with me on the edge. After my SNCC experience I have been disappointed, because I have not come into contact with people of such dazzling brightness" (O'Neal-McCray 2012:66).

Doug McAdam interviewed people who had participated in the 1964 Mississippi Freedom Summer voter registration drives. He found what I would call nostalgia in the lives of some of the Freedom Summer volunteers. One volunteer described her current life as "a totally unresolved tragedy." After Mississippi, she spent 12 years in another extraordinary experience as a member of the Communist Labor Party. She described both of these affiliations as enabling her to have a sense of purpose and community her present life was lacking. She discussed with McAdam the "extreme loneliness and lack of purpose in her life," and said, "'I'm living a lie and I just don't know how to undo it!'" (McAdam 1988:219). Another volunteer said, "'I'm not politically active . . . and I feel in consequence . . . a great loss, a kind of rootlessness, a lack of real orientation and identity in the world . . . because of the loss of that political anchor . . . I cannot in good conscience any longer make that identification (as an activist) in my own heart, and that's profoundly troubling and disorienting . . . if you've lived so many years bound up in that world . . . and felt that you knew what your life was about'" (McAdam 2012:218).

THE FOURTH STRATEGY: RENEWAL

Renewal is a strategy of rolling oneself into a different extraordinary experience (or at least a new sort of experience), with the hope, conscious or unconscious, of recapturing the positive emotions associated with the extraordinary experience one has left. The renewal sought is on the emotional level, rather than at the level of meaning and purpose, and the new experiences one rolls oneself into may or may not be similar in content to the previous extraordinary experience. Edward Tick, a psychotherapist, has written about this phenomenon in *War and the Soul,* a book about healing American war veterans from PTSD.

> War affects our physical, emotional, and spiritual dimensions with an intensity that produces the strongest "high" the soldier will ever experience. Afterward, some veterans become addicted to taking life-threatening risks in other settings. As one combat vet said, "I wasn't addicted to the killing but to the 'high.' Fights, drunken binges, automobile racing, and compulsive sex are a few means by which veterans attempt to replicate the high produced by war" (Tick 2005:222).

Marine Lance Corporal James Jenkins served two combat tours in Iraq. He was awarded a Bronze Star for valor in a fifty-five hour battle in Najaf in 2004. This fighting was nearly hand to hand, with Marines often only yards away from an enemy militia. When he returned from his second tour, he began gambling and got addicted to blackjack and pai gow. "The knife edge excitement felt comfortingly familiar" (Dobie 2008:11–12). I was told by returning war veterans I interviewed that some combat veterans re-enlist when they are unable to find satisfactory ways to repeat the high of war at home. Another example of renewal comes from a *Men's Journal* magazine report on an American college student from UCLA who joined the rebels in Libya fighting against Muammar al-Qaddafi. Leaving behind a paid summer internship at an asset management firm, he arrived in Libya and was taken in by a rebel group. He soon took part in a battle, and was exhilarated by the experience. He returned to UCLA for the fall semester, but felt distanced from his studies, and during spring break returned to Libya. At the end of the magazine article, he was looking for dynamite—planning to go out with some fishermen who fish by throwing dynamite into the water and harvesting the dead fish that float up. He described himself as craving instability and desiring to live in the moment (Davis 2012).

The strategy of renewal also occurs after non-military kinds of extraordinary experiences. Nando Parrado had a childhood love of cars, which on one level explains how he got into automobile racing soon after his return to ordinary life. But perhaps automobile racing was also one way to replicate the adrenaline rush that had to have been there to carry him over the mountain and walk another forty-five miles to safety when he escaped from the disaster in the Andes. When Doug McAdam interviewed people who had participated in the 1964 Freedom Summer voter registration drives in Mississippi, he found that they continued to be involved in political activities for years afterward, some seeking to renew positive emotions felt in Mississippi. One of these volunteers described himself as seeking to use the same "compulsive energy" he had exercised during the Freedom Summer. He felt he had finally found the same "electric" energy in an anti-nuclear project he led which incorporated "movement songs" and civil disobedience (McAdam 1988:215). Another volunteer who looked to recapture his Mississippi experiences visited Brazil, an Israeli kibbutz, Africa, and Central America; served as a volunteer in Vietnam; and was looking forward to his next experience, which he described as "the ultimate Mississippi." He planned to travel to seven countries and adopt orphans in order to create a diverse family of children from disadvantaged countries (McAdam 1988:229).

THE FIFTH STRATEGY: PSYCHOTHERAPY

Many returnees today turn to psychotherapists for help in sorting out issues involving identity, relationships, and purpose, especially if they are suffering from PTSD or related problems such as depression. Returnees also access self-help books written by people with expertise. Although there does not seem to be any type of psychotherapy that works for every sufferer from PTSD, there are a number that do seem helpful, and in affluent countries such as the United States, many returnees have pursued getting help from psychiatrists, psychologists, and social workers. As many as 40 percent of American veterans have been helped in this way (Rosenberg: 2012).

It is beyond the scope of this book to discuss all the PTSD therapies in detail, but they can be classified into two broad types: cognitive reprocessing, in which a person learns to think about the traumatic experience differently, and prolonged exposure, in which the person is helped to re-experience the trauma so as to become desensitized to it. An interesting therapeutic approach that seems to work for many people is EMDR, or eye movement desensitization and reprocessing. The idea behind this therapy, which I see as a combination of both types, is that rational talk and thinking are helpful, yet not sufficient to deactivate highly emotionally charged memories. This is because of the way that traumatic memories have become lodged in the emotional part of the brain. In EMDR, the patient's eyes follow blinking lights that scroll across a screen (or other versions of this) from right to left and left to right, while recalling traumatic events or episodes and responding to questions from the therapist. No one exactly understands how it works, but the therapy seems to help the brain re-store traumatic memories in the same way that normal memories are stored, without so much of the emotional intensity and vividness of the original experience. It also seems to help the person begin to recall positive as well as negative memories associated with the traumatic times. EMDR can also help people stuck in overly positive fantasies about their extraordinary experiences, to reprocess the memories in a more holistic way, so that they include the negative as well as the positive. The founder of EMDR, Francine Shapiro, has written a guide to the therapy for lay people (Shapiro 2012).

Therapists can even help returnees who went through traumatic experiences to actually *thrive* as they work to meet the challenges they face. Psychologists Richard Tedeschi and Lawrence Calhoun have coined the term "post-traumatic growth" to describe the idea that people can grow in positive ways from traumatic experiences. Tedeshi has asserted that post-traumatic growth is more common than PTSD, and that it can occur even in those suffering with PTSD. The possibility of growth occurs when people struggle to make sense of a traumatic experience. In a study of 600 trauma survivors, Tedeschi and Calhoun found that many had come away with improvement in five areas: appreciation of life, the ability to see opportunities, personal strength, relationships, and spiritual satisfaction (Rendon 2012).

Therapy can also be a stepping stone to pursue other strategies. I suspect that people are likely to pursue strategies seven, eight, and nine below if they have gained more insight into themselves through therapy.

It is unfortunate that therapy was unavailable for millions of people in the past who returned from extraordinary experiences, such as military combat, or incarceration in concentration camps and the *Gulag*. Eva Lukacs commented to me bitterly about the absence of any sort of psychological counseling in Europe for child survivors of the Holocaust. They were fed and housed, but no one helped them try to heal emotionally, even though they were still children, and often without surviving family members. It is all the more unfortunate that in the U.S., where therapists abound, therapy is still unavailable, due to the cost, or the stigma placed on seeking therapy for mental health issues.

THE SIXTH STRATEGY: PERSONAL HEALING PRACTICES

Some returnees use personal practices to heal themselves from emotional suffering. The first person to walk the full length of the Appalachian Trail, Earl Shaffer, was a veteran of World War II who had served in the South Pacific. Mourning the loss of his best childhood friend in the assault on Iwo Jima, his goal was to "walk the Army out of my system." Chris Hedges, the war correspondent whose story was told in chapter 1, wrote about Earl Shaffer as well as about Hedges' own healing through hiking in the mountains in the northeastern United States. When Hedges was working as a war correspondent, he returned to the mountains year after year, saying that he "drove" himself as he hiked. "I brought with me the stench of death, the cries of the wounded, the bloated bodies on the side of the road, the fear, the paranoia, the alienation, the insomnia, the anger and the despair, and I threw it at these mountains . . . To know the forests and mountains were there . . . gave me a psychological and physical refuge." On one trip in the White Mountains, he met a campsite caretaker who was an Iraq War veteran. The veteran said, "You try and forget the war but you carry pieces of it with you anyway . . . In the mountains, at least, I can finally sleep" (Hedges 2010). A similar approach was taken by a World War II prisoner of war, Ken Porwoll. Porwoll had survived several years of slave labor in Japanese prison camps and suffered from tuberculosis of the spine. He sought to heal himself physically and spiritually by going for walks: "Every day I walked. I would walk three or four hours a day by myself. Listening to the birds and looking at the flowers and absorbing the peace around me . . . I would get up on the knoll and look down over the lake and watch the sunfish come up and take the bugs off the lily pads and all that . . . Sometimes I would sleep out all night on the beach" (Saylor 2007:246–47).

Religious practices offer an approach to personal healing when they help a person shift attention away from troubles and difficulties. The phenomenon of *attention* is emphasized in various Asian religions and psychology, and a good deal of psychological research supports the idea that a person's quality of life is strongly influenced by what a person pays attention to (Gallagher 2009). The ToDo Institute in Vermont, which teaches Japanese psychology, offers a course on "Working With Our Attention" that shows people how to practice and improve their ability to pay attention. People can learn to shift their attention away from negative interior thoughts and feelings, memories about the past, worries about the future, and complaints about other people, to the environment around them, what is happening in the present moment, and gratitude for how others are supporting them. Substituting a pleasing for a disturbing thought is suggested in *Vipassana meditation,* a form of Buddhist meditation that seeks to help people become more detached from all passing thoughts and emotions so that they become more mindful of the present reality and can live more peacefully in it (Gunaratana 2011). In Western religions, as well, prayer can be used in this manner. One returnee told me that although he was not especially religious, when he felt anxious or fearful, he often found himself reciting the Bible's Twenty-Third Psalm. He had learned the words as a child during some now forgotten period of religious training, and they had seemingly, out of the blue, come to his mind again when he was having painful memories. "The Lord is my shepherd, I shall not want, he maketh me to lie down in green pasture, he leadeth me beside the still waters, he restoreth my soul . . ." The repetition of these phrases over and over was remarkably soothing. Now when he recites the psalm, he also visits over and over again in his mind, images he has created of the green pasture, and the still waters.

Another type of personal healing practice is the pursuit of education. Judith Clark was a radical activist in the 1960s whose exit from that extraordinary experience landed her straight in prison. During this second extraordinary experience, she was able to reinterpret her activist past, and become a healthier person than she had ever been in her life. Judith Clark had been sentenced to life in prison for driving a getaway car for the 1981 robbery of a Brink's truck, which resulted in the deaths of two guards and two policemen. She was a member of a radical spinoff of the Weatherman group called the May 19th Communist Organization. She was one of four people charged with armed robbery and murder. Others have been released, but Clark has remained behind bars in part due to the unrepentant and militant behavior she exhibited as a young woman at the trial. An acquaintance from childhood interviewed Clark for a story in the *New York Times*. Clark told Tom Robbins that she had lived a self-destructive life before prison and, "In prison, I learned who I was." Early on in serving her time, she spent two years in solitary confinement for plotting an escape. During that time, she "consumed books on psychology." She thought about her child and the children of the men she had killed. She was a new mother at the time of the robbery, and had visits with her daughter even when in solitary. She began to connect with her child during those visits; her daughter was "the first person I fully engaged with on her terms, not on what I thought was right or my agenda." Clark also reconnected with her Jewish faith and during the Jewish High Holy Days one year, she read out the names of the men who had died in the robbery. At that time, she was grieving the death of her own father, "And yet, there were nine children who were a lot younger than me grieving for their fathers. And I was responsible for that. There was the human toll. It was a terrible truth, but it was my truth." She eventually began to pursue formal education, earning a B.A. in behavioral psychology and a M.A. in psychology. Today other inmates credit her with helping them on their own journeys of self-discovery, and understanding their need to take responsibility for their actions (Robbins 2012).

THE SEVENTH STRATEGY: SUPPORT FROM OTHER RETURNEES

This is a strategy that connects a returnee with others who have gone through similar experiences. Returnees meet to share stories, listen, and provide help of various kinds, especially emotional support. Judith Herman writes in the context of PTSD, "the restoration of social bonds begins with the discovery that one is not alone." Support groups have helped survivors of traumatic experiences in combat, political persecution, rape, incest, and battering. Some therapists form support groups for their patients. Herman classifies these groups into several stages: the first is concerned with the issue of safety; the second with the traumatic event, and coming to terms with it; and the third with the survivor's re-entry into relationships with ordinary people (Herman 1992:215, 217). But seeking the support of others is not a strategy confined to trauma survivors, or a strategy only organized by therapists. For example, workers in the Civil Rights Movement formed support networks after the Movement had waned; former prisoners connect with one another through churches and community agencies; exonerated death row prisoners connect with one another through advocacy organizations; and veterans connect with one another through groups like the Veterans of Foreign Wars, Iraq Veterans Against the War, and a variety of other networks. One veteran described how he was helped by other veterans:

> I am so lucky to have the network of friends in Iraq Veterans Against the War I can call on. I know that if I ever need help or support, or if PTSD is driving me crazy that I can call on friends who know exactly what I'm going through and who can help me and talk me through the worst of times. I love all you guys and you should all be proud of the family and community that we've created within IVAW. We are the hope for countless waves of Iraq War Veterans, and we will be there for them, just as we're there for each other (Blake 2006).

Edward Tick has written about the importance to war veterans of sharing stories. In *War and the Soul*, he makes the point that there is a difference between "telling war stories" for the purpose of rekindling the adrenaline (which falls within the strategy I have termed "renewal"), and sharing one's war experiences for the purpose of *"healing the soul."* According to Tick, PTSD among soldiers is more than a psychological disorder of the brain caused by extreme stress, it is also a disorder of the "soul." By soul, he means the spiritual and moral dimensions of the person. War leads to a "moral inversion," among both soldiers and civilians, in that "in order to kill, one must invert one's sense of good and evil. Afterward, having betrayed their ethical codes when they had to, they cannot tolerate the betrayal. They feel trapped in moral dilemmas they cannot resolve in any acceptable way, and the impasse breaks the soul" (Tick 2005:113). Tick encourages veterans to share their stories with one another. He also leads "reconciliation retreats," in which veterans share their stories, not only with one another, but also with non-veterans present. Included in Tick's philosophy is the idea that the entire society must accept responsibility for sending the soldiers into a situation that will force them to live in moral pain. There is an alienation in our society between soldiers and civilians that must be bridged. To do this, Tick also advocates restoring traditional "warrior ethics," which emphasize life-affirming values over violence and death—values such as protection of life, peacemaking, controlling violent tendencies, fearlessness, and service to spiritual and moral principles (Tick 2005:251 ff.).

Societies sometimes place barriers in the way of returnees supporting one another. In New York State, for example, parolees are forbidden to associate with others who have a criminal record. Doing so may result in their being sent back to prison. The justification is that other ex-cons may tempt them to return to criminal activities. Thus parolees may interact in authorized therapeutic settings, such as a halfway house, but spillover friendships can get them into trouble with the authorities (Heinlein 2013:41–42, 5–6).

THE EIGHTH STRATEGY: POLITICAL ACTION

Political action involves telling one's story to the public, with the purpose of winning people over to take action of some kind. For example, many Vietnam War veterans returned home to create a GI Movement that opposed the war and raised public awareness about its brutality and senselessness (Zeiger 2005). Some of the survivors of the Soviet *Gulag*, as we have seen, returned home to oppose the Soviet system. In regard to PTSD, Judith Herman speaks of "survivor mission," and sees this as an important way of redeeming the trauma. A survivor mission involves raising public awareness: in order to help fellow survivors, or to prevent future victims, or to achieve justice

(1992:207–11). In developing a survivor mission, a person usually creates a powerful narrative about one's life before the extraordinary experience, the horrific nature of the experience, and the present commitment to the cause of making sure this does not happen again. Some survivors have achieved international recognition for their missions; for example, Elie Wiesel received the Nobel Peace Prize in 1986 for his Holocaust memoir, *Night,* and other works, and his activities to ensure justice for victims of the Holocaust. In his acceptance speech, he said that he was working to ensure that the memory of the Holocaust was not erased, and that people will understand that wherever there is suffering, we are responsible to speak out, and to take sides (Wiesel 1985:117–20).

Without returnees pursuing political action, it would have been harder to write this book, because I have used memoirs written by returnees who had the goal of raising public awareness about their extraordinary experiences. Several of the people whose stories were told in chapter 1 share this goal and it will be worthwhile to summarize here some of the kinds of political activities they have engaged in. Ishmael Beah, the former child soldier, published *A Long Way Gone: Memoirs of a Boy Soldier* in 2006 when he was twenty-six years old. He immigrated to the United States at the age of eighteen, finished high school at the United Nations International School, and later graduated from Oberlin College. Beah's life has been one of an activist seeking help and justice for child soldiers. According to the book jacket for *A Long Way Gone,* he is a member of the Human Rights Watch Children's Rights Division Advisory Committee. He has spoken before the Council on Foreign Relations, the Center for Emerging Threats and Opportunities at the Marine Corps Warfighting Laboratory, and many other NGO panels on children in war. He has also published articles on the issues. Chris Hedges, the former war correspondent, published *War is a Force That Gives Us Meaning* in 2002, as the U.S. "War on Terrorism" was gathering steam. The message of the book is clear: our culture, like many others, glorifies war, and many of us believe it gives meaning to our lives. Yet war is incredibly destructive. Hedges ended his work with a meditation on death (Thanatos) and love (Eros). Freud had regarded these as the two essential instincts of humans; he believed that the conflict between love and death characterizes all civilization. Hedges wrote, "To survive as a human being is possible only through love . . . love, in its mystery, has its own power. It alone gives us meaning that endures. It alone allows us to embrace and cherish life (2002:184–85).

As discussed in chapter 1, Primo Levi vowed while still in Auschwitz, to write about the experience. He had a powerful desire to share the experience with others and believed that he survived in the camp in part because of his intent to live in order to write about the experiences (1985:9, 377, 397).

Shelly Bermanzohn states in her book, *Through Survivor's Eyes,* that she originally entered a political science Ph.D. program with the goal not only of possibly having a career, but also "as a chance to work out my own political understanding of what had happened to us" (2003:337). Bermanzohn began with a Ph.D. thesis for which she interviewed fifty-three people who had been in the Greensboro march on the day it was attacked by the KKK. Then she wrote her book, which is based on the testimony of some of the survivors of the attack, a sort of collective memoir, including her own story. Bermanzohn has also been associated with an organizing effort to achieve justice in the city of Greensboro. An Epilogue to her book publicizes the goals and activities of the Greensboro Truth and Community Reconciliation Project, organized with the help of the International Center for Transitional Justice (ICTJ). The ICTJ has helped local people start reconciliation projects around the world. According to a spokesperson for ICTJ cited in Bermanzohn's book, the Greensboro project is the first such project to be city-based rather than nation-based, and may become a model for other cities. I will say more about this project in the next chapter.

Even memoirs cited here which might seem just a personal story, reflect a mission. Nando Parrado's *Miracle in the Andes* ends by urging the reader to "realize what treasures you have" (2006:284). Ron Kovic stated in *Born on the Fourth of July*, that he finally began to realize that he could "come back," and that he had the power to change people's attitudes about the war (1976). In an Introduction to a new edition of the book published in 2005, Kovic wrote, "I now believe I have suffered for a reason, and in many ways I have found that reason in my commitment to peace and nonviolence . . . It is a blessing . . . to be able to reach such a great number of people" (2005:24). Kovic's book was a best seller, and a film based on the book won two Academy Awards.

The wars in Afghanistan and Iraq led to a substantial anti-war movement among troops and veterans in the U.S. Although little publicized in the mass media, it has been documented in a book by Dahr Jamail. Through veterans' houses, coffeehouses, websites, and other means veterans opposed to the wars have gotten together and spoken out. At a 2008 "Winter Soldier" national conference organized by Iraq Veterans Against the War over 200 veterans testified about the nature of the Afghanistan and Iraq occupations and urged the public to take a stand against the wars. Similar events were organized across the country (Jamail 2009).

The two child Holocaust survivors I interviewed have been working for years with a survivors' organization they helped found. The organization has been very active in publishing and public speaking. Anita Schorr is an inspiring speaker. In her eighties, she goes to middle schools, high schools, and colleges, to speak about her experiences. She draws a lesson for today's children in their own environment, urging them to stand up and be "heroes" when they witness bullying and other inhuman acts. A moving story of Schorr's childhood experiences for young readers, accompanied by discussion questions and a list of resources, has been written by Marion A. Stahl (Stahl 2014). An accompanying story of Schorr's later life is forthcoming, also by Stahl. As mentioned earlier, Schorr and Lukacs were drawn into this work through telling their stories to a university oral history project. By getting involved with this project, they met other survivors, and for the first time, they were finally being able to talk to other child survivors about their experiences. They went from being silent to having increasingly powerful voices in the community.

Some returnees distance themselves from their past and from fellow returnees. Instead of seeking public sympathy and support for themselves as victims or survivors, they criticize their past beliefs, activities, and fellow participants, in an effort to rally the public against the kind of person they once were. An example of this is Max Bitterman, one of the people interviewed by Vivian Gornick in *The Romance of American Communism.* Gornick described Bitterman as "the anti-Communist Communist." Max Bitterman had left the Party after twenty-five years. He became an author of an academic history of American Communism and a political science professor. In his interview with Gornick, Bitterman expressed his anger with the Party and fellow Communists, describing Communism as "the work of the devil." He expressed great scorn for people who had left the Party either before or after he did, because they had left for what he considered the wrong reasons (1977:210–11).

Another example of distancing from the past is David Horowitz, the child of Communist parents, and a 1960s New Left activist and author, who has written a memoir of his transformation into a conservative activist. Horowitz described himself as increasingly disengaged from the Left when he came to believe that the Black Panthers had committed serious crimes, including murdering members and supporters. He came to see people on the left, himself included, as guilty of standing by and doing nothing to prevent the crimes or to bring the perpetrators to justice. He also came to see this as part of a pattern of left disregard for rule of law and human rights, including the crimes of the governments of Stalin, Mao, Castro, and the crimes of leaders of North Vietnam, the Khmer Rouge in Cambodia, and the Sandinistas in Nicaragua, which he believed were in many ways downplayed by the Left in the United States. As his thinking evolved, Horowitz became a vocal and influential conservative critic of the Left and defender of the American system, which he saw as having a more real commitment to the rule of law and individual rights than its opponents (Horowitz:1997).

Taking an oppositional stance towards one's past affiliations is by no means confined to the Left. An example from the Muslim world is a former activist with an extremist Islamic movement, Maajid Nawaz. His memoir, *Radical: My Journey Out of Islamic Extremism* (2013) is an interesting account of his path to Islamic extremism and ultimate turn against it to become one of the founders of a London-based institute that works to counteract extremism. Nawaz grew up in London, the child of Pakistani immigrants. As a teen he experienced violence from racist skinheads and discrimination by the police; he was radicalized, first by the oppositional messages of American hip hop music, and then by an Islamist organization called Hizab Al-Tahrir. This organization analyzed problems such as those Nawaz had encountered as the result of a global oppression of Islam by Western colonialism and imperialism. It sought to establish a Muslim Caliphate in the mostly-Muslim nations, not by jihadist-style violence initiated by the group's members, but by winning over the militaries of these nations, which would then seize power through military coups.

Nawaz became a leader in the organization and traveled to Pakistan and other countries in an effort to recruit other youth to its mission. This was an extraordinary experience which culminated in Egypt with a four year prison sentence. In prison, he met other activists from a variety of persuasions and over time began to question the leadership of Hizab Al-Tahrir and ultimately its ideology. He was also influenced by John Cornwall of Amnesty International, which had taken him on as a "prisoner of conscience," since Nawaz's arrest was simply for his beliefs, and not for any violent actions. After his exit from prison, Nawaz returned to England and eventually left Hizab Al-Tahrir. Nawaz and another ex-Islamist, Ed Husain, founded the London institute, Quilliam, named after an Englishman who founded the first mosque in England. Quilliam is dedicated to spreading a "counternarrative" to radical Islamism within Muslim communities, and promotes the ideals of "respect for basic human rights, pluralism, individual freedoms, faith and democracy" (Nawaz 2013: 212). Founding such an institute was quite controversial and Nawaz stated in his book that "most Islamist organizations from all branches of Islam" came to see them as enemies. "At once, all my friends had turned on me, and I lost so much. Apostate, I was called. Hypocrite. Traitor. Sellout" (Nawaz 2013:222, 248). Yet Nawaz has been able to move on with this work and has extended his network to Pakistan and other countries.

THE NINTH STRATEGY: RECOGNITION OF CONTINUITY

This is a strategy in which a person grasps that there is a continuity of the self and identity before, during, and after the extraordinary experience. This continuity may be expressed in a narrative that they tell themselves and others. This is an achievement requiring, in my view, a strong sense of self, and perhaps also a strong ability to reflect upon that self even amidst extraordinary experiences that may engulf others at the same time and place. It differs from renewal in that renewal is an effort to recapture positive *emotions* associated with the extraordinary experience, while recognition of continuity is about a person's overall identity, values, and purposes in life before, during, and after the experience.

A striking case is Diane Vinson, the blacklisted actress discussed in chapter 3 who was interviewed by Vivian Gornick in *The Romance of American Communism*. Gornick describes her as someone who has spent her whole life, including her years in the Communist Party, "alive with the dramatic pursuit of self-knowledge" (1977:228). Vinson was born and raised in a poor family in Kentucky, and escaped poverty by going away to college. In college at Kentucky State, she fell in love with acting and later became an actress, eventually in New York City. There, she was influenced by a Russian immigrant coach, who taught her about Marxism, and its ideas of class struggle and class consciousness. Her coach had left the Soviet Union because he had felt stifled there, yet he inspired in Vinson an excitement for a Marxist perspective on the world. Suddenly she could understand and feel anger at the poverty suffered by her family on the farm in Kentucky. From her perspective as an actress, she could also see class conflict as the "drama of the ages." She joined the Communist Party and dedicated her life to being both an actress and a Communist Party member. Both of these roles involved activities that were enabling her to express herself, understand herself, and to grow. Eventually she left the Party after a number of years, when it became increasingly clear to her that she was no longer learning and growing. She began to notice that everything personal was "suppressed and despised" by the Party, which contradicted her tendency to see everything through her own personal vision and sense of self. After leaving the Party, she became director of an acting company and went to graduate school to study psychology, continuing her pursuit of self-understanding.

Vinson expressed little regret for having been a Communist. She was glad that she had "learned from the Party the tragedy of identifying your entire self with anything outside of yourself." But she also was glad she had learned "the depth and height of human aspirations" and how those aspirations "take on a shape that forces you to identify with things outside yourself." She saw it as tragic, the contradiction between the desire to grow as a person, and the desire to change the world by being identified with something outside yourself. At the time of her interview with Vivan Gornick, Vinson was able to view her entire life as cut from the same piece of cloth: "My years as a Communist were born out of my need to experience myself, and they ended out of the same need. I could return to the theatre with new strength, new knowledge, new independence, and work within it better than ever. I could be myself, and still act. I could not be myself, and still be a communist" (Gornick 1977:233–34).

Other stories about continuity reflect a continuity of values before, during, and after the extraordinary experience. Maajid Nawaz, the returnee from Islamist extremist experiences, eventually came to see that it was a passion for justice that both led him into radical Islam, and out of it, toward democratic ideals (Nawaz 2013:191–92). Penny Patch, the civil rights organizer whose story was discussed in chapter 1, had joined the Civil Rights Movement because she did not want to be a bystander in the face of what she saw as evil. Eventually she became a midwife in rural Vermont. In the movement to help women "take control of their own birth experience" she found continuity with values of human empowerment that she felt were realized in the Civil Rights Movement (Curry et al. 2000:138, 166). Joan C. Browning, also discussed previously, saw both her time in the Civil Rights Movement and her later life as outgrowths of her belief that as a Christian she should be a "witness to spiritual values." She now lives in a community she loves and is active in various efforts to improve the community (Curry et al. 2000: 81–82). *Hands on the Freedom Plow*, a collection of dozens of personal accounts by women who were involved in SNCC, shows that many of the women went on to engage in pursuits that expressed values they had before and during the Movement (Holsaert 2012). As one contributor, Joanne Christian Mants, put it, "The Movement continues wherever you find yourself" (Mants 2012:139). The same theme is apparent in several life stories told in *Want to Start a Revolution? Radical Women in the Black Freedom Struggle* (Gore 2009).

Doug McAdam found a similar theme in his interviews with Freedom Summer volunteers. The vast majority stated that their values had not changed since Freedom Summer. One volunteer continued to work with a variety of issues, with a common thread being her desire for achieving "participatory democracy" ("let the people decide"). Another spoke of a quest for creating community and of his work done later creating new "beloved communities." It is interesting that over half of the volunteers ended up in professions involving service to people, such as education, social services, legal, and medical fields (McAdam 1988:214, 225, 226).

Karen Armstrong, the British ex-nun, finally understood after decades that there was continuity between the girl of seventeen who had entered the convent and the writer on theology she had become in her middle years. In her second memoir, Armstrong described herself as unsuccessful or unfulfilled in several ordinary career paths she chose after leaving the convent. She had studied for a doctorate in literature, worked as a schoolteacher, and produced television documentaries. Eventually she began writing books about theology and during this time she finally realized that she would never be like everyone else, with a normal career, marriage, and children. Following Joseph Campbell, she came to believe "we have to 'follow our bliss,' and find something that totally involves and enthralls us, even if it seems hopelessly unfashionable and unproductive, and throw us into it heart and soul" (Armstrong 2004:305). She found a special passion in writing books about non-Western religions such as Islam and Buddhism, with the goal of helping people in the West to understand these traditions. Inspired by the T.S. Eliot poem *Ash Wednesday*, Armstrong likened her journey to climbing a narrow "spiral staircase." She realized she had attempted to get off her narrow staircase and be on "what seemed to me to be a broad, noble flight of steps, thronged with people. But I kept falling off and when I went back to my own twisting stairwell I found a fulfillment I had not expected" (Armstrong 2004:306). She described herself as climbing and turning, recognizing that she could never go back and be the person she once was before she joined the convent; yet as she was climbing and turning, she was always getting more insight into herself. She found similarities between what had drawn her to life in the convent, and her current life as a writer: "I tried to break away from the convent, but I still live alone, spend my days in silence, and am almost wholly occupied in writing, thinking, and speaking about God and spirituality. I have come full circle . . . as I go up, step by step, I am turning again, round and round, apparently covering little ground, but climbing upward, I hope, toward the light" (Armstrong 2004:306). Linda Nelson, the former nun I interviewed, seems to have taken a similar path in terms of recognizing the continuity of her life. Initially drawn to be a nun in an order that had missions in the developing world, she had sought a life that united spirituality with service to others. She continued that service through church work, and hopes to one day write about her experiences and beliefs.

EVALUATION OF INDIVIDUAL STRATEGIES

In this overview of the nine strategies, I have pointed out along the way that some of them are accompanied by ongoing emotional stress. While some strategies are ways of getting to the goals of reconstructing the self and identity, reinterpreting the extraordinary experience, and developing new relationships with others, they may or may not result in a great deal of personal satisfaction or happiness. In this section of the chapter, I take a look at the effectiveness of the strategies in relation to satisfaction or happiness, and try to identify which ones work better, and why.

Repression and Silence/Secrecy

The strategies of *repression*, and *silence/secrecy* are probably the *least* successful in meeting the challenges and achieving a measure of satisfaction or happiness in life. Repression, and silence/secrecy are directly aimed at dealing with the challenges of return, but their success is superficial on a psychological level. While either of these may enable an individual to cope with material survival and safety, and go about daily life, they do not enable an individual to meet the personally deeper challenges of reconstructing the self and identity, reinterpreting the meaning of the extraordinary experience, and developing satisfying relationships with others.

Repression of memories may not even be achievable. In the case of trauma, as we have seen, memories break through to consciousness despite efforts to repress them. They also show up in the form of nightmares. As we have also seen, even if repression succeeds, a person may have great difficulty in personal relationships. Finally, it may go without saying that meeting the challenge of reinterpreting the meaning of the extraordinary experience is impossible when one is seeking to forget about it altogether.

I want to mention in this context that in the U.S. a kind of collective repression is often urged upon African Americans with regard to the legacy of slavery. African Americans are told that slavery is "in the past," and that they should forget about it and "just move on." Joy DeGruy has made an important counterargument to this in *Post Traumatic Slave Syndrome: America's Legacy of Enduring Injury and Healing* (2005). She points out that experiences during slavery and Jim Crow were traumatic for many African Americans, and that today's racism continues to provide traumatic experiences. The effects of trauma have also been passed down from one generation to the next. DeGruy argues that healing can only happen when history is fully examined.

Silence/secrecy, like repression, can also result in a great deal of emotional pain. At first glance, secrecy/silence may seem a bit better than repression, since the person is relieved of the struggle to forget what happened, however, it is not comfortable to be a person with an inauthentic or false self. As we have seen, one's sense of self is confused, and relationships with others are unsatisfactory because there are areas of the self that cannot be revealed. True intimacy is impossible. This includes intimacy regarding what is meaningful in life. Silence/secrecy is also an obstacle to reinterpreting the extraordinary experience in the light of the present. Reflections that might otherwise be shared with intimate others, become an interior, mental pursuit. In all these ways, silence/secrecy also undermines a quest for satisfaction or happiness in life. Moreover, silence/secrecy, like repression, can have negative emotional effects on the next generation. Arlene Stein's *Reluctant Witnesses: Survivors, Their Children and the Rise of Holocaust Consciousness,* is a fascinating report on her research into this phenomenon among the children of Holocaust survivors. The rise of "Holocaust consciousness," she argues, has its origins in part from the quest of the next generation to fill in the painful and puzzling gaps in family memories (Stein 2014). Unfortunately, when the social context is sufficiently hostile and punitive, silence/secrecy becomes the strategy of choice for many returnees. It may be that the price to pay for an authentic self and deeper relationships with others is just too high.

Renewal

Renewal, or seeking to recapture positive feelings from the extraordinary experience by plunging into another kind of experience, avoids altogether many of the issues of return to the ordinary world. While the person may survive, and have a new sense of self, that sense of self is not connected to the ordinary world. The person has not really learned to go about everyday life, and his relationships with others in the ordinary world suffer as they take second place in the person's scheme of things. Renewal is not an effective strategy to meet the challenges of return. It may seem so to the person involved, but that is an illusion.

Nostalgia

In the case of *nostalgia,* the individual is filled with pleasant memories of the extraordinary experience, and life in the present seems pale or meaningless in comparison with the thrilling past. Despite reflecting on the past, a person in the state of nostalgia does not fully meet the challenge of reinterpreting the past in the light of the present. The positive memories may be a fantasy, since in all likelihood the extraordinary experience, like most experiences, was neither all good or all bad. It was a mixture of good, bad, and indifferent. What is being remembered is an incomplete picture of the experience. Also, like the strategies of repression, and silence/secrecy, on a superficial level, the person may be meeting the various challenges of return to the ordinary world, but the person is not engaged on a deep level with the self he has created and the people he is in relationships with in the ordinary world. In this case, the self is not false, it is just not fully present. Psychological research has indicated that the kind of comparisons we make have a great deal to do with our levels of satisfaction or happiness. If we compare ourselves with others who are better off, we feel negatively about ourselves. If we compare ourselves with others who are worse off, we feel positively about ourselves (Wills 1981:245). This seems to imply that comparing one's current self with an illusory happy past self is not a recipe for happiness.

Some researchers have speculated that nostalgia can have some positive functions. For example, Ebaugh, referring to research by Davis, suggested that nostalgia provides a sense of continuity in life, of a strong identity, because in remembering the positive, and forgetting the negative, a person feels that they dealt successfully with life in the past, and therefore will continue to do so in the future (Ebaugh 1988:173–74; Davis 1979:33). This may be the case for non-extraordinary experiences, however I did not find examples of this in returnees from extraordinary experiences who lived in a state of nostalgia.

Psychotherapy, Personal Healing Practices, Support Groups, Political Action, and Recognition of Continuity

The strategies of *therapy, personal healing practices, support groups, political action (including survivor mission) and recognition of continuity* all involve a greater amount of self-reflection as compared to the other strategies just discussed. They often involve conscious reflection on one's whole life, before, during, and after the extraordinary experience. Because of this, they seem to offer better chances for establishing an authentic self that is engaged and present in the ordinary world and relationships with others, and a self that is clear about its purposes in life. As such, these strategies are more likely to result in personal satisfaction or happiness than repression, secrecy/silence, renewal, and nostalgia.

The strategies of *political action (including survivor mission)* and the *recognition of continuity* seem to me to have an *additional* advantage: they offer the best chances for enabling a person to achieve a state which is called *"constructive marginality"* in the literature on intercultural communication. The term constructive marginality was coined by intercultural communication experts Milton and Janet Bennett. "Marginality" is a term that has long been used to characterize those who have crossed from one cultural world to another (e.g., immigrants, or people who enter the mainstream after growing up as a member of a racial or ethnic minority). Because such people have stepped out of their culture of origin, they are no longer like the "normal" people in that culture. Yet because they are newcomers to the new culture, they are not completely accepted by the "normal" people in that culture either. Historically, the "marginal" person has been depicted as a powerless and unhappy character, an outsider. But the Bennetts point out that marginality is not necessarily a negative state. It can also be experienced and utilized positively, or constructively (Bennett 2000). In "negative marginality," the person is no longer at home in either culture; he or she may be unhappy and depressed, and unable to form good relationships with others. The person has not fully learned the new culture and adjusted to it, nor has he or she fully accepted that it is not possible to simply go back home again. In contrast, in a state of "constructive marginality," the person has learned to deeply understand and communicate in the new culture, and has a good practical and theoretical grasp of how culture shapes the individual. As a result, he or she manages to become comfortable and at home in both the culture of origin and the new culture. What is "constructive" in constructive marginality is not only this positive state of mind, but also that the person is able to act in his or her community to help build bridges between the different cultures. Being at home in both, the person is able to effectively explain one culture to the other in a way that others may not. Such a person is thus uniquely positioned to help promote better cross-cultural understanding and to help prevent and resolve conflicts between the two cultures (Bennett 1993, 2000).

Like immigrants or members of minority groups in the mainstream, returnees from extraordinary experiences will be "marginal" for the rest of their lives, if only because many people in the ordinary world may never fully accept them as being just like themselves. Thus the choice is not between being marginal or being "normal," but between enduring marginality in a negative way, or embracing it in a constructive way. Therapy, support groups, and personal healing practices may not necessarily deal with this situation. But both political action (including survivor mission) and the recognition of continuity are strategies that clearly and completely embrace the inevitable marginality and turn it to more constructive use. In political action (survivor mission), the returnee is bridging the gap between survivors and the "normal" people by explaining the extraordinary experience to the "normal" people in a way that only a survivor can explain it. Yet in the process of explaining, they are re-learning how to communicate in the ordinary world and are becoming comfortable enough in it to be able to have a dialogue with people in it in the ordinary way. They come to be seen by people in the ordinary world as a fellow human being who happens to have extraordinary qualities which are admirable. The same is true of those using a continuity narrative. The experience of continuity functions like a survivor mission, although on a micro or private level. Such a person lives in the ordinary world as someone who is different, but is able to communicate, in an ordinary way, about that part of their past that is different. They also come to be seen by people in the ordinary world as a fellow human being who happens to have extraordinary qualities which are appreciated.

The advantages of the "better" strategies may seem obvious. But what if the social context is hostile or punitive? In a hostile world, an individual will inevitably be confronted by people who believe their extraordinary experiences mark them as having a deeply flawed, even evil or criminal character. To achieve satisfaction or happiness in life, a person must become equipped to endure and rebound from these inevitable contacts with people who stigmatize them. That may be more difficult than it appears, since these interactions may take the harsh forms of physical attack, deterioration of an intimate relationship, or imprisonment. It may be impossible to pursue open political action, or speak openly about the continuity of one's experiences. When a previously positive context turns harshly negative, a person may choose to retreat from open healing endeavors into the strategy of silence/secrecy. Conversely, when the social context is supportive and welcoming, the best strategies will be reinforced, and more returnees will be able to pursue them.

In the next, and final, chapter, I discuss public policies towards returnees. I will share some of my thoughts on supportive policies and programs that seem to me to be needed in order to promote satisfaction or happiness.

Chapter Six

Implications for Public Policy

This closing chapter is an overview of public policies and programs needed to help returnees. Although one individual strategy for dealing with the challenges of return may be better than another, I have concluded that it is also important to recognize that sometimes even the best individual strategies have limited utility. If the social context of the returnee is hostile and punitive, then even the best individual strategies cannot be maximally successful. Fortunately, the converse is also true. Positive public policies and programs can also be helpful. In the course of my research, I came across some examples of supportive public policies and programs, which will be discussed below. I hope these inspire returnees and their supporters who are working for improvements. I also hope this information will promote more public dialogue about the need for such programs. I believe that good policies and programs not only benefit individual returnees, they also benefit local communities and society as a whole. As mentioned in the Introduction, societies in the world today face the task of incorporating literally millions of returnees, and the failure to do so contributes to many social problems. For example, in the U.S., many released prisoners fail to find jobs, commit new crimes, and are returned to prison; some of the soldiers returning from repeated deployments to wars in Iraq and Afghanistan have been violent toward others, or suicidal (Schaller 2012). It seems likely that societies that help returnees meet the challenges they face will be safer, healthier, and more productive. Programs to help returnees succeed are also cost-effective; it is well known that it is more expensive to imprison and hospitalize people than it is to educate them and/or prevent them from getting sick.

In the following pages, I address this issue of the social context and how it can be made more positive for returnees. I discuss the general nature of policies and programs I see as needed to help returnees meet the challenges of return. I address the issue of stigma. I highlight some examples of good initiatives.

RECOGNITION OF ALL CATEGORIES OF RETURNEES

Some categories of returnees have a recognized legal status in some countries and there are public programs in place to assist them. In the U.S. and many other nations the statuses of military veteran, parolee, refugee, and (in some cases) disaster survivor are recognized, and there are benefits attached to these statuses. Refugees around the world also receive help from the United Nations. As is well known, the benefits are not adequate, but returnees who are looking for help can at least identify and access some benefits, and returnees have organized into advocacy groups to press for improvements.

Around the world, particular circumstances have given rise to legal recognition of other categories of returnees. Demobilized combatants have been recognized and are entitled to some forms of assistance in countries such as Colombia, El Salvador, and South Africa that have undergone civil wars and revolutions. Freed slaves are recognized and assisted in some countries in the developing world and the industrial democracies. Again, the services available for such returnees are not adequate, but the status is at least recognized and the services identifiable.

Other categories of returnees lack a legal status with benefits attached to it. That does not mean that they are totally without support, but it is more ad hoc and less institutionalized. In the U.S., some former undercover agents and war correspondents have employers and/or professional associations that look out for the interests of their members and may provide some very limited aid for returnees, ranging from posting information and advice on a website to insurance coverage for therapy. Exonerated death row inmates and people who have left unusual religious groups have gotten together with supporters and created organizations to help returnees and advocate for beneficial public policies and programs. Other categories of returnees, such as former revolutionaries, former aid workers, and people exiting from social movements, seem less likely to have even this rudimentary form of assistance (Hughes 2015).

All categories of returnees should be recognized and assisted. If there are already organizations in place that might logically provide help, such as employers or professional associations, these organizations need to provide assistance if they are not already not doing so. If there are advocacy groups, the rest of us could be more proactive in extending a helping hand. Despite the undoubted psychological and social benefits of the "survivor mission," it is shameful that survivors have to spend so much time and energy advocating for themselves. Survivors would be freer to choose their paths to happiness if the rest of us provided more immediate recognition and assistance.

Another source of recognition and assistance is the existing governmental and community agencies that provide services relevant to returnees. If they are not already doing so, they can reach out to the un-served and underserved categories of returnees such as exonerated inmates, returnees from unusual religious groups, social movements, or former aid workers. For example, the mandate of organizations serving ex-prisoners could be expanded to include the exonerated. Mainstream churches could make it clear that they welcome people leaving unusual religious groups, in the same way that many currently advertise themselves as welcoming congregations for gays and lesbians, or refugees. Community agencies with therapeutic services could clearly advertise that returnees are one of the populations they welcome and serve. Government agencies providing aid to people in transition such as the unemployed could also clearly advertise that returnees are one of the populations they help. People out of the national labor force for many years because they were working overseas or in a social movement would be more likely to seek them out.

Over the long run, perhaps it is not too farfetched to suggest that a universal status of "returnee" be recognized, with rights and supportive benefits attached to it. Perhaps assistance with return from extraordinary experiences should be seen as a human right that should be written into the United Nations Universal Declaration of Human Rights, and incorporated into legislation at national and local levels. In the U.S., for example, this might begin at the State level, particularly in States that have already been receptive to the needs of certain categories of returnees, such as parolees or freed slaves, or have demonstrated willingness to support other human rights issues such as environmental preservation and voters' rights.

Of course, not every returnee needs the help that could come with recognition. Those who are wealthy and psychologically resilient, with excellent support networks, may not need assistance. But this should not excuse us from recognizing returnees in general and assisting the many who *do* need help.

POLICIES AIMED AT REDUCING STIGMA

Returnees who face stigma and discrimination are always swimming upstream in a quest to return to an ordinary life and find happiness in it. Stigma threatens returnees' ability to meet all of the challenges faced, from material survival and safety to establishing relationships. To make matters worse, there is also a stigma attached to certain kinds of help, such as psychotherapy. This is especially strong in the U.S., a culture where even elderly or unemployed people are often ashamed to ask for food stamps let alone seek treatment for mental health problems. A RAND Corporation survey of American veterans of Iraq and Afghanistan found that one-third reported post-traumatic stress disorder (PTSD), depression or a traumatic brain injury; of those with serious depression or PTSD, only half had sought any treatment (Rosenberg: 2012).

I recommend one simple strategy for reducing stigma that everyone can implement immediately: individuals and institutions can begin to use neutral language to refer to returnees. For example, prisoner advocate Eddie Ellis has suggested that released prisoners be referred to as the "formerly incarcerated," rather than "ex-offenders," "persons on parole," and other terms with negative connotations (Gray 2013:5–6). I would suggest "returnee" as a neutral term that covers many situations.

In general, the best way to reduce stigma will be to publically recognize the status of returnee and establish adequate programs to help returnees deal with the array of challenges they face. When "returnee" is a recognized status with the right to receive needed benefits in an atmosphere of respect, that will go a long way towards lessening the stigma presently attached to some categories of extraordinary experiences. Recognition and benefits will send a message that returnees are human beings like everyone else and that it is expected that they will be welcomed back into their nation, community, and family. It will correct the stigmatizing attitude that there is something inherently wrong with returnees or that since they may have voluntarily chosen to have an extraordinary experience, they should just "suck it up."

What kind of benefits do returnees need? In the following pages, I will present my vision of what is needed, and some examples of good policies and programs from around the world.

BENEFITS NEEDED BY RETURNEES

An Interim Guarantee of Short Term Material Survival and Safety, and Help in Learning How to Navigate in the Ordinary World

Housing, food, health care, etc. should be provided during a specific transition period to those who lack sufficient resources of their own. During this period, returnees can begin to learn how to find their way in the ordinary world with the help of trained counselors or mentors. Assistance should include help in learning how to use contemporary technology, finding work and educational opportunities, and getting information about changes in cultural values, norms, and laws. The length of the term of assistance should depend not simply on available public resources, but also on individual situations; some returnees may only need help for a month, others may need help for years.

Examples of such programs exist on a partial basis for certain categories of returnees, but should be widely available for all who need them. A few examples will demonstrate the advantages of such programs, not only to the returnee but also to the rest of the community and society.

A successful program for the formerly incarcerated exists in Seattle, Washington. As has been seen in this book, the formerly incarcerated in the U.S. face stigma when attempting to find housing and jobs. Pioneer Human Services in Seattle operates a program that provides not only housing, jobs, and other services, but also a workshop for those who are hard to place in regular employment options. It is a nonprofit that funds itself almost entirely through the businesses it operates rather than grants and donations. The majority of those served manage to stay employed either by Pioneer or in the job market, and Pioneer claims that the recidivism rate of participants is only 5 percent (Petersilia 2003:198).

The Anti-Slavery Movement has given much attention to what is termed the *rehabilitation* of freed slaves, understanding that it is not sufficient to simply free a person from slavery. When slaves are liberated they need a lot of assistance to make the transition to the ordinary world. The challenge of meeting the need for material survival was highlighted above in chapter 4. But much more is needed. A manual on best practices has been published by Free the Slaves, a nonprofit organization operating worldwide to try to eliminate modern day slavery. Written by Helen Armstrong, *Rebuilding Lives* discusses the need for transitional shelter accompanied by the provision of a large variety of services including food and water; medical care; psychosocial help; "activities that calm and heal;" and the skills of daily living. The manual also recommends that the freed persons should be taught about their human or civil rights; protected from punishment or deportation; and helped to plan wise ways to spend any compensation money that might be given them by government (Armstrong 2008). Agencies offering transitional shelters and other services exist around the world. In the U.S., particular attention has focused on young women rescued from sexual slavery. The Polaris Project has estimated that in the U.S. in 2012, there were a total of 529 beds available in shelters exclusively for sexual trafficking survivors (Polaris Project). Free the Slaves has produced a comprehensive report on organizations sheltering and rehabilitating former slaves in four developing nations: Cote d'Ivoire, Haiti, India, and Togo. The report covers dozens of organizations offering a wide variety of services (Hyde and Bales et al. 2006).

A Guarantee of Help in Reconstructing Self and Identity, Reinterpreting the Meaning of the Extraordinary Experience, and Establishing Relationships

Psychotherapy

Psychotherapy should be available with therapists especially trained to work with returnees. This should be available not only to those with trauma, but also to those simply confused or adrift and needing to talk with someone in order to sort out their thinking. Helpful therapists and therapies are abundant in the U.S. and other industrial democracies. Even a cursory look at the situation will show that at present the issue is not so much availability as access for those with limited resources along with the problem of stigma. Both availability and access for people in the developing world are limited.

It would be helpful if more therapists were trained in the general issues of returnees. At present, to my knowledge, therapists are not trained in this way. Instead, they may have expertise in trauma issues, or in helping specific categories of returnees such as war veterans or cult survivors. An education and certification process could be established that addresses the more general nature of extraordinary experiences and the return process.

I do not mean to present psychotherapy as a panacea. There are schools of psychotherapy that attribute great importance to early childhood experiences in forming personality. As a result, some therapists who work with returnees have actually avoided discussing their extraordinary experiences and steered discussion back to childhood events. This happened to the British ex-nun, Karen Armstrong, for example (Armstrong 2004:123). Moreover, some therapists are more skilled than others, and not every returnee is open to psychotherapy. Legal issues can hamper therapy. For example, if therapists must report client disclosures about past crimes, returnees may not be open about their pasts (National Public Radio 2015). Therapy must also be made available with sensitivity to the cultural context. Psychotherapy is an unfamiliar practice in the cultures of many developing countries, and there is controversy over whether and how it should be offered. For example, in some African countries, former child soldiers often state that their biggest need is to see a traditional healer who can cleanse them of the spiritual pollution they took on during war. Former soldiers are told after purification ceremonies not to "look back" lest bad spirits return, so talking with a counselor can be seen as unsafe. Stigmas against mental illness also exist. About 10 percent of former child soldiers may be so traumatized that they need psychotherapy. But it will not be accepted unless there is sensitivity to the social and cultural context (Wessells 2006:194, 201–202).

Alternative Healing Practices

Alternative medicine practices should also be available. This includes practices such as mindfulness, meditation, yoga, tai chi, qi gong, breathing, biofeedback, and self-expression through drawing, journaling, or dance, etc. The American military has been using alternative practices for veterans with PTSD, with some excellent results reported. The Center for Mind-Body Medicine in Washington has created a program in which veterans can choose among many of the variety of practices just listed (Rosenberg 2012). Mindfulness, which originated in Buddhism, is seen as one of the most promising. As discussed in chapter 5, a person learns to focus the attention on the present moment rather on the ever-shifting and not always positive thoughts and feelings that constantly run randomly through the human mind. Alternative medicine practices have certain advantages over psychotherapy. They lack the stigma attached to psychotherapy. These are practices that are increasingly popular among the general public, making them more accepted. They are seen as skills we can all learn, not as something only for a person who is severely troubled. These practices can also be taught by lay people, thus vastly expanding availability. The Center for Mind-Body Medicine, for example, trains 1500 people a year to lead groups in one of its courses. The American military has begun to use the Mind-Body programs at some of its VA hospitals, bases, and at the National Intrepid Center. VA researchers in Minneapolis found that 80 percent of participants showed improvement (Rosenberg 2012).

The U.S. anti-war movement has also created alternative healing projects for veterans. For example, as discussed by Jamail (2009), the Warrior Writers Project seeks to provide "tools and space for community building, healing and redefinition." Veterans attend workshops at which they write and produce artwork centered on their experiences in the military, and they are sponsored to travel around the country to read and show their work. The Warrior Writers Project joined with another organization to create the Combat Paper Project, in which veterans learn how to use the cloth of their uniforms to produce paper, which they then transform into works of art or use in writing projects (Jamail 2009:189–93).

Public Education Campaigns

Public education campaigns are another possibility. As seen throughout this book, returnees may be reluctant to ask for help from a therapist or even to communicate with family and/or friends. Public education campaigns should be targeted at raising awareness about the challenges faced by returnees, reducing the stigmas attached to mental illness and psychotherapy, and changing ideas such as the assumption that therapy is only for the mentally ill. A precedent exists in the sort of campaigns that have already sought to lessen the stigma attached to seeking help for depression. These campaigns have explained what depression is, outlined symptoms, and made the point that depression is an illness for which treatment is available today. There is a hopeful message that recovery from depression is possible, even likely. New campaigns to reduce the stigma of mental illness more generally are currently in the works in the United States, prompted by public concern over the mass shootings at the Sandy Hook elementary school in Newtown, Connecticut, in 2012. The White House sponsored a National Conference on Mental Health, which called together mental health activists, political leaders, and religious leaders to discuss ways to reduce the stigma of mental illness. At the conference, President Obama called for mental illness to be brought "out of the shadows." Campaigns are reportedly beginning that target youth and veterans, including one program that will post information about mental health services on Internet message boards visited by people who play video games (Somashekhar 2013; Runningen 2013). A similar campaign could be done for returnees from extraordinary experiences. Factual information could be presented about the kinds of extraordinary experiences that people go through and the challenges they face when they return from them. Testimonials of returnees could be incorporated into the messages. The point could be made that it is a sensible and effective strategy to seek the support of trained consultants. The American military's National Center for PTSD has already begun an educational campaign of this sort, called AboutFace. AboutFace consists of an online video gallery of veterans talking about their problems with PTSD and how they have gotten better, portraying them as just people like the rest of us. Media kits are available to members of the public who want to help publicize the site (Rosenberg: 2012; AboutFace).

Public campaigns could also ease the stress on returnees by helping people in the ordinary world better understand how to relate to them. As seen throughout this book, returnees may be reluctant to talk to family and friends about their experiences; family and friends in turn may be clueless about how to start a conversation. There can be no authentic relationships for returnees unless they can be more open about their experiences with at least some intimate friends, spouses, or family members. Such openness also paves the way to enable more returnees, and society, to benefit from constructive marginality, in which returnees become bridge builders between the ordinary community and the culture of their extraordinary experience. A public education campaign could explain the benefits on both sides when bridges are built. It could make others more aware that returnees might like to talk about their experiences, given an interested and non-judgmental ear. Such a campaign would also explain how to express a welcoming attitude without being intrusive when a returnee does not want to talk.

Restoration and Reconciliation Programs

In addition to programs aimed at individuals, such as individual therapy and public campaigns to change individual attitudes, there are programs at the family, local community, and national levels that can help returnees in their struggle to reconstruct the self, reinterpret the meaning of the extraordinary experience, and establish relationships. Such programs can help in lessening stigma as well. *Restoration* programs function to return the person to an ordinary and accepted status in the community. *Reconciliation* programs go beyond this and attempt to achieve understanding between the returnee and the others in the community they have been in conflict with and may have harmed in some way. As we have seen, some extraordinary experiences are highly political or involve deeply felt moral matters—as in the cases of soldiers and participants in social movements or revolutions. Participation is controversial, and members of society are often negative or divided about the meaning of the experience. Rather than repressing the conflict from collective memory, which allows it to fester, reconciliation programs help everyone to process what has happened and go forward more peacefully to the extent possible. Both returnees and community members on all sides are aided in sorting out the issues in a safe and supportive environment. Sometimes these are called "*truth* and reconciliation" programs, the idea being that if everyone understands the truth behind what happened, it will be possible to forgive one other, or at least have some empathy for one another and move on with less tension and conflict. It is heartening to see the growth of reconciliation programs in response to genocides and wars, and also to see that they are beginning to connect with one another internationally. Such connections may further the emergence of an "ethic of remembering," whereby human empathy on a global scale can help prevent new genocides and wars (Stein 2014:177–82).

Restoration and reconciliation initiatives exist around the world at a variety of levels—national, community, and interpersonal. There are some good programs that have originated in certain nations for specific categories of returnees; these should be adopted internationally and also adapted for other categories of returnees, where relevant.

Restoration: In some European countries, the formerly incarcerated are allowed to live down their pasts. After a certain amount of time has passed, if the person has not committed another felony offense, they are eligible for a legal status of "rehabilitated." In England, for example, people who have not received prison sentences of longer than two and a half years can go through a rehabilitation period of two and a half to ten years depending on their age and the length of their prison sentence. Once the time period has passed, a rehabilitated person acquires the same legal status as a person who has never been convicted of a crime. Their conviction is considered "spent," and the person no longer has to mention it when asked in job applications, civil proceedings, applications for insurance, public benefits, and housing. (Certain jobs are exempt: one's prison record must still be mentioned if applying for jobs working with children, the elderly, or in criminal justice.) England's laws are actually stricter than those of other European nations. In most of them, *all* criminal records become spent after certain time periods. This enables the returnee to construct an identity in the ordinary world without the cloud of stigma faced by the formerly incarcerated in the United States (Petersilia 2003:217–18). It also supports one of the better individual strategies, the "recognition of continuity" in one's life. Shadd Maruna has found that the formerly incarcerated who "desist," i.e., who do not return to a criminal life, tend to see a continuity in their lives. Referring to Turner's concept of the "real self," he describes how those who desist see themselves as basically good persons who got on the wrong path, and through their prison experience and rehabilitation have managed to get back to being the kind of good person they always were. This has been called a *redemption script* in the field of narrative psychology (Maruna 2001:85–108; Turner 1976; Bruner:1987).

In the very different cultural setting of Liberia, after its civil war ended mothers began to reach out to former child soldiers, children who were not their biological children. All over the country, child soldiers began a trek home, often stopping on the outskirts of the villages from which they had been kidnapped years before, and which they had perhaps even attacked during the war. In one small village, when the war ended, children began to live under a tree on the edge of the village, but would not come into the village due to their shame over what they had done. Villagers began to call it the "Tree of Frustration." Over time, mothers began to come to the tree. They would leave food, then stay and eat with the boys and talk with them. At first they did not talk about the war at all or try to push the boys to come home. They would talk about their ancestors, the community, and sometimes prayed or sang. It became a shared space where they could simply be together again, villagers and boys. Finally, after relationships had developed, they asked the boys to return, and the boys agreed to do so. At the same time, they created a kind of redemption ritual to prepare the boys for return. The children were dirty and had long unkempt hair that had been growing unwashed for years. The women began to cut the boys' hair in "an act of reintegration and love." Hair cutting is something mothers traditionally do for children in Liberia. By doing this, the mothers were saying to the boys that they could be children again, they would be accepted as children again by the community. "A weight far greater than hair fell from the boys' shoulders; the mothers hands and scissors spoke: 'We forgive you. We want you to come back and be our sons'" (Lederach and Lederach 2010:147–48,159–66). Similar rituals of return have occurred in other African countries, according to Wessells (Wessells 2006:197–99).

Reconciliation: In Sierra Leone, after its civil war was over, there was a kind of collective silence about the war in some villages. Young women who had been child soldiers took the initiative to break the silence and reconcile with other villagers. Miriam, a young woman who had borne a child after being raped and taken to be a soldier, went home to a village that was less than welcoming. She was taken through ritual cleansings, but the village still refused to let her live there with her baby, or to allow her to go by her birth name. Other young women who returned felt deeply ashamed and did not want to talk about what had happened to them. Somehow Miriam persuaded the chief to allow her and other young women returnees to put on a play about the war. For the play, each girl told her own story, but indirectly by creating a character with the same story. This enabled them to speak without shame. The play was very effective. It showed how everyone had been hurt by the war. People cried, including the chief (Lederach and Lederach 2010:186–90). Lederach and Lederach, who are international peace builders, make the point that when returnees give voice to their experiences through poetry, drama, music, and dance, there is a much greater depth of feeling than when reconciliation is attempted through processes such as formal interviews. They advocate what they call "social healing" at the community level, using aural media and direct engagement, to supplement reconciliation processes at national levels that may be more impersonal.

The International Center for Transitional Justice has helped people organize truth and reconciliation projects in many countries including Bosnia-Herzegovina, Afghanistan, Sierra Leone, Mexico, Peru, and East Timor. Their first project in the U.S. was with the community of Greensboro, South Carolina, the site of the KKK attack on civil rights marchers discussed earlier in this book. The goal in Greensboro was to uncover the truth about what had happened in the attack, help the community come to terms with the injustices done, and make recommendations about how the community should go forward. A Commission was formed in 2004. Although the city government decided not to endorse the Commission, there was widespread support among the public. The Commission held several days of hearings with testimony from victims and other witnesses, and over 400 people attended the first hearing. The Commission also interviewed over 200 people. In 2006, the Commission issued a report on its findings, with a variety of recommendations. It proposed that the community formally acknowledge, apologize for, and commemorate the attack; reform various institutions, such as government, criminal justice, and the media; introduce diversity education into these institutions; and create methods for other citizens to take part in diversity education. One analyst familiar with truth and reconciliation projects has concluded that the Commission was a success in "meeting the aims of acknowledging and clarifying the truth, responding to the needs and interests of victims, and promoting reconciliation and reducing tensions." The Commission's report was officially received by forty-seven government and community groups. It was also utilized in educational efforts by churches, museums, and schools. As an unofficial body, the Commission could not punish perpetrators or achieve legal redress for victims, however "if justice is thought of as accountability to one's community, then the work of the Commission was effective in this regard." Victims were especially moved when members of the community showed support for them by holding a re-enactment of their proposed march route, and when one of the perpetrators apologized to them during one of the hearings (Hansen 2007).

Edward Tick, author of *War and the Soul*, has been leading reconciliation trips to Vietnam since 2000. His groups include military veterans, their families, educators, activists, and students. They visit battlefields, shrines, schools, and healing centers. Tick involves civilians because he wants to help diminish the alienation in the U.S. between citizens and soldiers. As mentioned in chapter 5, he believes that everyone in a nation has responsibility for war, not simply the soldiers or the government. He also believes that civilian life can be improved if there is more appreciation of the structure and discipline of the warrior. The warrior's ethic, attached to peaceful goals, would be an "extraordinary synthesis" (Schimke 2008). Tick has written about the welcoming attitude of the Vietnamese his groups have encountered on their journeys. "The numbers of Vietnamese people killed, wounded, missing, displaced, homeless and disabled during the Vietnam War far exceeded ours. Their ecology and infrastructure were ravaged, while ours was untouched. How disarming it is, then, for Americans to find Vietnamese welcoming them as honored guests and offering friendship and forgiveness—while many at home still quake in terror of how we might be treated around the world" (Tick 2005:268). Tick also holds reconciliation retreats in the U.S. attended by small groups of Vietnam veterans and nonveterans, including Vietnam era anti-war activists. The men share their stories of the Vietnam years; honest communication is fostered by passing around a "talking stick," a practice of indigenous peoples that commits the person who holds the stick to speak the truth as he sees it, and everyone else to listen with an open mind. In a description of one such retreat, Tick wrote about how the men came to feel themselves to be part of a team. "These men were now brothers, old friends. They had received each other's broken youths, honored each other's struggles and choices, respected each other's differences, and balmed each other's wounds. Fourteen men, who had arrived having never told their stories to men who were different, left feeling newly a part of a team, a generation, a history, and a shared story" (Tick 2005: 224–234).

HELP THAT RESPECTS INDIVIDUAL REALITIES, INDIVIDUAL AUTONOMY, AND INTEGRITY

Help needs to be provided in a way that respects the autonomy and integrity of individuals and an individual's actual situation. Unfortunately, in some societies, people in the ordinary world may create rigid expectations about the process of returning from the extraordinary. They may expect that all individuals must or should, in an identical fashion, reconstruct the self and identity, reinterpret the meaning of the extraordinary experience, and establish relationships. As mentioned earlier in the book, Jerry Lembcke has made the argument that Americans increasingly view veterans as victims afflicted with PTSD and in need of medical and psychiatric help. A stereotypical "one size fits all" social construction of this sort places blinders on returnees and other members of society. Another example comes from Sierra Leone and the return of child soldiers. As Susan Shepler writes in her interesting account of former child soldiers, *Childhood Deployed: Remaking Child Soldiers in Sierra Leone* (2014), there is a narrative constructed by UN agencies and international NGOs that child soldiers were "just children," innocent victims of adults who coerced them into war, and whose innocence can be restored with adult forgiveness and re-entry programs providing psychosocial activities inducing the returnees to become children once again. This social construction has made its way into Sierra Leone through various helping agencies, and many former child soldiers have come to adopt its rhetoric to explain themselves. Yet Shepler's investigation found that there are also children who "self-reintegrate" without going through an agency and adopting the child-victim construction. These children manage to navigate a return to ordinary life, and in some cases, seem more successful at it than the children who were involved in re-entry programs.

Rigid social constructions of reality may be inevitable in human cultures; certainly there are enough examples in human history when many people have believed that witches, or Communist agents, were everywhere. Public programs can, however, create some built in safeguards to protect individual realities, individual autonomy, and integrity. For example, there is the promising practice of "Non-Violent Communication" (NVC) that promotes deeper communication among individuals in organizational as well as private settings. NVC involves techniques for listening in an open way to a person's expressed feelings and needs, whether or not they match up to prevailing social constructions or the views of the listener (Rosenberg 2003; Connor and Killian 2012).

LESSENING THE GAP BETWEEN THE EXTRAORDINARY AND THE ORDINARY, AND ELIMINATING SOME EXTRAORDINARY EXPERIENCES

If the gap between extraordinary and ordinary worlds were not so large, it would be easier for returnees to return. In certain situations, something can be done about this. Some extraordinary experiences do not need to be as exceptional as they are. When they are under public control, it is within our power to change them.

The Missouri prison system has implemented a strategy called "Parallel Universe" developed by Dora Schriro, former Director of the Missouri Department of Corrections. The approach is based on the idea that prisons should be as much like ordinary society as possible and that inmates should be helped to develop the values, habits, and skills needed to function successfully in ordinary society upon release. The inmates are engaged all day in activities that mirror what people do on the outside—work or go to school for a full day, go to appointments for medical or mental health treatment, engage in community service, recreation, etc. Inmates are interviewed for their jobs and are encouraged to keep them by following directions and modifying behavior in response to evaluation. Non-high school graduates can improve their pay if they earn a GED. Inmates are also given more responsibility in personal matters than is typical in many American prisons. They keep track of account balances at canteens, renew prescriptions before they run out, and make decisions about when to do laundry and clean their cells, etc. Missouri reports that the Parallel Universe model has reduced recidivism. The percentage of released prisoners who return to prison went down from 33 percent in 1994 to 20 percent in 1999. Missouri's recidivism rate is one of the lowest in the United States (Petersilia 2003:183).

A similar strategy has been adopted at the only women's prison in Hawaii. When Mark Kawika Patterson took over as warden, he noticed that 90 percent of the women had been sentenced for drug offenses and a third of them were on medication for psychiatric problems. Of the prisoners with addictions, 75 percent had a history of emotional, physical, or sexual trauma. Yet there were no mental health professionals on the staff. The vast majority of the 270 prisoners were classified as minimum security, but all of them were treated like the minority who were higher security. Patterson began to work to change the prison to be more like a community-based healing center than a prison. Facing budget cuts, Patterson brought in community volunteers to create helpful programs. A local conservation group helped create hydroponic gardens and train inmates in growing vegetables, which are used in the prison kitchen. An instructor from a local community college teaches culinary arts and inmates can earn certificates, which help them get jobs upon release. Children are allowed to visit on weekends and volunteer counselors from a local nonprofit agency mingle with the families and coach the mothers, when needed, in better parenting. In the future, Patterson hopes to transform the prison courtyards into gardens (van Gelder 2011:38–39).

Natural disasters are another arena where we can diminish the gap between the extraordinary and ordinary. The idea of disasters such as hurricanes, floods, and fires being "natural" conceals the fact that human societies can do much to prevent and mitigate their harmful effects, and to assist survivors in an adequate way. A well-known negative example—Hurricane Katrina in 2004—can make the point. This was a catastrophic disaster that did not need to have happened in the way that it did. When Hurricane Katrina hit New Orleans in 2004, the city was woefully unprepared. Its system of levees was inadequate to prevent severe flooding of most of the city from even a level 2 hurricane, which Katrina had become by the time it hit. The city had no plan in place to evacuate residents without transportation, leaving its high percentage of poor, African-American, and elderly people trapped in flooding homes and unsuitable shelters. At the convention center that had been offered as a shelter, the power failed, and twenty thousand people suffered for many days without adequate sanitation, food, and water. Buses promised to take people out of the city after the storm did not come in a timely way, nor did the National Guard and other official rescuers. The nation and world outside New Orleans were shocked when media images began to appear of the large numbers of mainly African-American people waving for help from the roofs of their homes, wading waist deep in floodwaters, pushing sick and elderly people on improvised rafts, and facing hunger, sickness, and death in the heat at the convention center. Terrible stories emerged that some survivors were shot by vigilantes or police when they attempted to walk out of the city, and that personnel at a nursing home without power or water were faced with the choice of euthanizing patients or watching them suffer horribly.

The extraordinary experience of surviving Katrina, like other experiences discussed in this book, was not all negative. People found satisfaction, even joy, in reaching out to help one another. Where government had failed, volunteers stepped in. People from the City, State, and indeed from all over the country were inspired to reach out to help. Volunteers rescued people, took in the homeless, established ad hoc medical clinics, raised money, provided counseling, gutted and rebuilt houses, and performed countless other acts of kindness. Rebecca Solnit has written in *A Paradise Built in Hell* about the extraordinary joy and generosity that emerged in this, and other disasters. She argued that humans seem to have a deep hunger for connection and meaning in life that is met when we join together to rescue and rebuild. The positive emotions that result from this replace the negative emotions of fear and scarcity that are so prevalent in the everyday world. She urged us to consider trying to inspire that joy and generosity in efforts to *prevent* future disasters, and to deal with other *ongoing* social problems, such as poverty and injustice (Solnit 2010:231–304, 312–13; Fink 2009; Lee 2006).

Social movements call for some extraordinary experiences to simply be eliminated. The international peace movement promotes nonviolent conflict resolution and an end to war (Olson 2014). The United Nations and many nations have prohibited slavery and the enlistment of children as soldiers. The U.S. Civil Rights Movement calls for an end to racism in the criminal justice system and the mass incarceration of African-Americans and others.

Some countries curtail groups that exert too much power over participants. Some extraordinary experiences occur in organizations such as religious groups, political organizations, and military forces which deliberately use manipulative techniques in an effort to reshape the thinking of participants so that it is in line with the culture of the group. These techniques include restrictions on freedom of interaction with others in the outside world for longer or shorter time periods, combined with constant education about the group's world view (Lifton 1963:420–37). Such restrictions and education may be voluntarily accepted, but over time, a person may lose the ability to think critically. (This used to be called "brainwashing," but current thinking among researchers is that this term fails to recognize that participants are not a blank slate but are often voluntarily seeking the kind of information being imparted.) A person may end up staying in the organization because they can no longer view their situation with any objectivity. In the U.S. and other democracies, freedom of association is seen as a civil right or human right. This has often been interpreted in such a way as to give religious, political, and military organizations a great deal of free rein over participants. Religious groups have from time to time even gotten away with outright violent coercion in addition to subtle manipulation. Some countries have recognized that there is a contradiction contained in the principle of "freedom of association" and that organizational freedoms should not be allowed to trump individual freedoms. Germany, for example, has restricted Scientologists, and neo-Nazi groups. Other nations might want to give more consideration to this issue. Manipulative techniques should be banned. At the very least, there should be a greater amount of public education regarding the meaning of "freedom of association," such that citizens learn about manipulative techniques groups may use (even groups that may be approved of by the authorities and general population) and understand what is involved in critical thinking. It should be clearer that freedom of association does not give groups the right to undermine individual autonomy, whether the techniques they use are subtle or coercive.

MAKING IT HAPPEN

I hope readers will share my vision of what is needed to assist returnees, and will become involved in helping to make it happen. Existing programs do not cover enough returnees, or provide enough help. They need to be greatly expanded and strengthened. Readers can get involved with advocacy organizations that are working to improve the situation of a category of returnees included in this book. Such organizations advocate for public policy changes, and a also provide immediate assistance to returnees. They can be found in local communities, and also on national and international levels. These organizations need volunteers, money, and publicity. With persistence, most of us can find an organization that appeals to us and choose a way to help that is consistent with our time and resources. Another way readers can make a difference is by "becoming the change you wish to see in the world" (an idea expressed by Gandhi, the leader of India's revolution against colonialism). Many of us will have opportunities to reach out to individual returnees we come across in our lives—to express an interest in their extraordinary experience, be kind to them if they are struggling, and be helpful in other ways consistent with our resources and lifestyles. Readers are likely to find that their lives have been enriched by having new friends who have been through extraordinary experiences. The best approach may be to *both* get involved with advocacy groups and to reach out to individuals—for as seen throughout this book, "exiting the extraordinary" is a social issue, not simply an individual one.

Appendix A

Methodological

INTERVIEWEES

All of those interviewed have been given a pseudonym, with the exception of Anita Schorr, who has become a public figure (See Stahl 2014).

Anita Schorr: child Holocaust survivor
Eva Lukacs: child Holocaust survivor
Cameron Smith: Army veteran (Iraq)
Andres Beaumont: Marines veteran (Iraq, Afghanistan)
Joe Gardner: National Guard veteran (Afghanistan)
John Nowak: veteran of a European Army (World War II)
Mark Alessi: aid worker
Linda Nelson: former nun
John Lerner: State Police officer

INTERVIEW FORMAT

Each interview lasted about two hours. In some cases, I scheduled a second session because I needed to clarify some points or because the person's story simply took longer to unfold.

I used an interview schedule with open-ended questions, covering the person's life before the extraordinary experience, the experience itself, and the person's life upon returning to the ordinary world. Subsequently, I coded the interview notes looking for themes I had already identified in the memoirs and other readings, and looked to see if any additional themes had emerged.

Participatory research has always interested me, and I endeavored to incorporate aspects of this into the interview process. In particular, I sought to engage the respondents in a collaborative way. I explained the purpose of the book to each person and invited them to give me their insights on the topic more generally. I asked them at the end of the interview whether they thought there were additional questions or topics that I should have covered, and kept a record of anything that came up. As mentioned in the introduction, I also asked them if they could refer me to other possible interviewees. I invited them to read drafts of the manuscript. Four of the people I interviewed read an earlier version of the manuscript and gave me their feedback on it. I feel very grateful to the people who allowed me to interview them about their life experiences. As their journeys unfolded to me, I felt honored and humbled by being in their presence. My commitment to this participatory process also led to some glitches. One elderly person I interviewed wanted to read the manuscript before consenting to have the interview information utilized. Unfortunately by the time the manuscript was ready, the person had became too ill to participate. As a result, I was unable to include information from the interview.

The people I interviewed were very interested in the topic, and expressed appreciation for being invited to share their experiences. I feel this reinforces the point made in chapter 5 that those who reflect on their lives have a greater chance of finding satisfaction or happiness in the ordinary world, whether this be by means of a therapeutic process, sharing one's story with others, joining with others in political action, or discovering a continuity in one's sense of self over the life course.

OTHER INTERVIEWS AND DISCUSSIONS

In the course of the research, I discussed the topic with two other people whose perspectives helped me clarify my understanding of the nature of "extraordinary experiences." Both of these people who had gone through experiences that were unusual, but not quite as extreme as the categories I included as the basis for developing my ideal type definition of "extraordinary experiences." In one case, I had interviewed the person before I had gotten completely clear about what I meant by "extraordinary experience." The other case was a person in my network of friends and family who had volunteered to read a draft of the manuscript and give feedback. These discussions were very helpful as I was struggling to figure out which categories of experience to use in developing the ideal type definition of "extraordinary experiences."

Appendix B

Theoretical

FOR CHAPTER 1

Experiences Included as Basis for Developing Ideal Type Definition of Extraordinary Experiences

As mentioned in chapter 1, there are experiences that others might consider "extraordinary" that I did not include in the list of types of experiences I used in order to develop the list of common characteristics of extraordinary experiences. People who read various drafts of the manuscript asked me about why I did not include former astronauts, actors in long running musicals, members of Congress, gang members, anthropologists, or other social scientists who had unusual field experiences, homeless persons, patients in drug rehabilitation centers, etc. I explained in chapter 1 that I did not include these sorts of collective experiences for the most part because I decided to create a model drawn from the more *extreme* experiences. As explained in the Introduction, a primary purpose of the book is to illuminate the process of returning to the ordinary world. By examining the more extreme experiences, I believe we see a greater number of the dimensions involved in the return process and see them with the greatest clarity.

There are two other types of experiences I did not include. I did not include unusual experiences undergone by individuals alone, such as being lost in the wilderness, having a near-death experience, or believing in alien abduction. These are worthy of investigation, but because they have somewhat different dynamics from experiences that happen in a collectivity, I believe they merit a separate study. I also excluded the experiences of people who have left extraordinary experiences having never known any other way of life. It is not really a "return" if one has never been in the ordinary world. For example, a young escapee from a North Korean prison camp never lived anywhere except the prison camp, because he was born and raised there (Harden 2012). Similarly, in the form of *chattel slavery*, people are born into the condition and have never known anything else (Bales 2000:19–20).

I also excluded unusual experiences that are manufactured for profit. Nowadays many people have planned transformative experiences as a result of taking part in "reality" TV shows like *Survivor*, or wilderness adventures. Although a fascinating topic—extraordinary experiences as a commodity, these experiences have somewhat different dynamics than "real" experiences, so I chose to stick to "real" experiences not planned for profit.

Extraordinary Experiences and Deviance

One reader of my manuscript questioned why I needed to coin the term "extraordinary" when the term "deviant" might serve just as well. To explain my reasoning, I need to briefly outline my perspective on the way "deviant" is commonly understood in the social sciences. Social scientists see the broader culture of a nation as a dominant, or hegemonic culture, which is reinforced or supported by powerful institutions. From the perspective of members of the dominant culture, some groups are deviant because they seem to violate important norms, values, beliefs, etc. of the dominant culture. Members of the dominant culture often label, stigmatize, and punish members of deviant subcultures for flouting the ways of the dominant culture. Social scientists who study deviance often include *some* of the kinds of experiences I am calling extraordinary. For example, social theorist Michel Foucault has written about "heterotopias"—an enigmatic term he used to refer to "those different spaces," "those other places," which includes such varied places as prisons, rest homes, and psychiatric hospitals ("heterotopias of deviance"); orphanages, boarding schools, and places where women give birth ("crisis heterotopias"); as well as places like cemeteries, gardens, fairs, vacation resorts, motels, and museums (Foucault 1987). However, as defined here, extraordinary experiences cannot be simply equated with deviance. Being a soldier in military combat, a war correspondent, an undercover agent, a victim of a natural disaster, or an aid worker in a developing country are not necessarily experiences that are deviant in the usual sense of the term. In fact, in the dominant culture, they may be considered just the opposite— praiseworthy, heroic, or ideal.

What is the "Ordinary World?" *Is* There an "Ordinary World?"

In this book, the meaning of "ordinary" is established in relationship to "extraordinary," as "extraordinary" was defined in chapter 1. The "ordinary world" in the sense of this book is the cultural world a person inhabited before leaving it for an extraordinary experience. It is relative to time and place; there is not *one* "ordinary world." The ordinary world of the Soviet *Gulag* survivor and the ordinary world of the American soldier returning from Afghanistan are two different realities. But both are ordinary in relation to the extraordinary worlds of the *Gulag* and the war zone in Afghanistan. The closest social science term for "ordinary world" might be "mainstream culture." However, some returnees may have originated in a culture considered a deviant subculture from the perspective of mainstream culture, so the term "mainstream culture" does not quite fit.

The terms "ordinary" and "extraordinary" are used here analytically. As outlined in chapter 1, I created an ideal type definition of "extraordinary experience" drawn from extreme experiences. The meaning of the words "ordinary" and "extraordinary" are of course also "socially constructed" by people in everyday life. It would be interesting to research what is seen as ordinary or extraordinary by members of different cultures and subcultures. In the U.S. today, people apply the term "extraordinary" to all sorts of experiences and objects, and usage does not always overlap with the definition in this book. Products and vacations, for example, are praised as "extraordinary" in television commercials. Some clues into what people think are "extraordinary experiences" can be found in a recent psychological experiment and the media reports on the experiment. The researchers wanted to find out whether coveted "extraordinary experiences" give people the happiness they are seeking, or whether they have social costs. The researchers divided subjects into groups of four and created a scenario in which one subject would have an extraordinary experience, defined as something unique and enjoyable, and the others would share what was defined as a more mundane experience. One subject watched a four-star rated video on a street magician, and the others watched a two-star rated animated video. Afterward, subjects engaged in conversation. It was discovered that the person who watched the four-star video (who had the more extraordinary experience) felt excluded from the discussion (Cooney 2014). Media reports on the research stressed the implication that there may be social costs of choosing to have extraordinary experiences that set one apart from one's peers. Perhaps one should think twice before pursuing unique experiences; perhaps one will have more friends if one does what everyone else does. One media report listed bungie jumping, zorbing, and mountain climbing as examples of "extraordinary experiences" (Mathews 2015). Another media report used the examples of going to a bar with Jessica Alba, sky diving, and Icelandic volcano spelunking (Khazan 2014). Another report used the examples of dining privately with Ben Affleck, taking a joy ride around town in a Lamborghini, or taking a great vacation (Hoffman 2014). It is interesting that these examples tend to be individualistic and consumer- oriented activities consistent with life in the ordinary world, rather than the type of extraordinary experiences discussed in this book.

FOR CHAPTER 2

Definition of Culture

I am using the term *culture* in the all-embracing way it is often used in anthropology, to refer to all of the patterns of human behavior that are learned rather than genetically determined. In sociology, the term culture is often reserved for the more abstract phenomena of symbols, values, norms, beliefs, technologies, etc. while the term *social structure* is used to refer to patterns of social behavior that constitute positions (statuses) in society, such as roles, groups, organizations, social classes, etc. I believe that the all-embracing use is more suitable for the purpose of this book. Since the book is intended to be a broad overview of returning to ordinary life after an extraordinary experience, I have tried to pare the conceptual discussion down to only those concepts that are the most essential for an understanding of the topic.

Nature of the Self

The idea of the self as a construction has been criticized for being culture-bound, in the sense that it may be based on a dualism between self and other that is assumed in Western culture more than other cultures. Buddhism, for example, envisions the self as interdependent with others, rather than disconnected. There is an interesting theoretical discussion going on in sociology and other social sciences about this issue (Immergut 2014).

FOR CHAPTERS 4 AND 5

Challenges and Strategies

Westervelt and Cook (2012) confronted some of the same issues I have raised in regard to a couple of theoretical matters. Although we may have used different terminology, we are on a similar theoretical page, so to speak.

First, the question of whether the experience of returning is better characterized as responding to a variety of challenges, or as going through a series of stages. They seem to recognize that circularity is present when they address the strategies exonerated death row prisoners use to "cope with life after death row." For example, they say that coping is a "process" not a "stagnant state." "Survivors use numerous coping strategies . . . and try on new ones when others become less helpful or more problematic" (2012:139).

Second, the question of how to characterize the strategies used by returnees. Westervelt and Cook classify strategies pursued by exonerated death row inmates after their release as either strategies of "avoidance," or of "incorporation," highlighting the degree to which they proactively seek to bring their death row experience into their present life (135 ff.). This is similar to the distinction I make between strategies such as repression, secrecy, nostalgia, and renewal on the one hand, which are less successful in enabling the returnees to have a satisfactory or happy life in the present, and the more successful strategies of therapy, personal healing practices, support, political action, and recognition of continuity.

References

Aarts, Petra G. H. and Wybrand Op Den Velde. 1996. Pp. 359–77 in van der Kolk, Bessel A. et al. eds. *Traumatic Stress: The Effects of Overwhelming Experience on Mind, Body and Society.* New York: The Guilford Press.

AboutFace. www.ptsd.va.gov/apps/AboutFace/index.html.

Adler, Nanci. 2004. *The Gulag Survivor.* New Brunswick, NJ: Transaction Publishers.

Adler, Patricia A. and Peter Adler. 1991. *Backboards and Blackboards: College Athletes and Role Engulfment.* New York: Columbia University Press.

Adler, Peter S. 1975. "The Transitional Experience: An Alternative view of Culture Shock." *Journal of Humanistic Psychology* 15 (4).

Alexander, Michelle. 2012. *The New Jim Crow: Mass Incarceration in the Age of Colorblindness.* New York: The New Press.

Allport, Gordon. 1954. *The Nature of Prejudice.* Redding, MA: Addison Wesley.

Angier, Carole. 2002. *The Double Bond: Primo Levi, A Biography.* London: Penguin.

Applebaum, Anne. 2003. *Gulag: A History.* New York: Doubleday.

Armstrong, Helen. 2008. *Rebuilding Lives: An Introduction to Promising Practices in the Rehabilitation of Freed Slaves.* Washington, DC: Free the Slaves.

Armstrong, Karen. [1981] 2004. *The Spiral Staircase: My Climb Out of Darkness.* New York: Anchor Books.

Armstrong, Karen. 2005. *Through the Narrow Gate: A Memoir of Spiritual Discovery.* New York: St. Martin's Press.

Badger, Emily. 2014. "Why the Iraq War Has Produced More PTSD Than the Conflict in Afghanistan." *New York Times.* April 3.

Babbie, Earl. 1992. *The Practice of Social Research.* Belmont, CA: Wadsworth Publishing Company.

Bales, Kevin. 2000. *Disposable People: New Slavery in the Global Economy.* Berkeley: University of California Press.

Bales, Kevin. 2005. *Understanding Global Slavery: A Reader.* Berkeley: University of California Press.

Bales, Kevin and Zoe Trodd. 2008. *To Plead Our Own Cause: Personal Stories by Today's Slaves.* Ithaca, NY: Cornell University Press.

Barrios, Manuelita, n.d. *Role and Ex-Role: The Process of Leaving the Role of a Paramilitary.* Unpublished manuscript. School of Human Services: Universidad del Rosario, Colombia.

Beah, Ishmael, 2007. *A Long Way Gone: Memoirs of a Boy Soldier.* New York: Farrar, Straus and Giroux.

Beirich, Heidi, Wood, Laurie. 2012. "Paying the Price." *Intelligence Report* 147.

Bennett, Janet M. 1998. "Transition Shock: Putting Culture Shock in Perspective." in *Basic Concepts of Intercultural Communication*, edited by Milton J. Bennett. Yarmouth, ME: Intercultural Press.

Bennett, Milton J. 1993. "Towards a Developmental Model of Intercultural Sensitivity" in *Education for the Multicultural Experience*, edited by R. Michael Paige. Yarmouth, ME: Intercultural Press.

Bennett, Milton J. 2000. *A Developmental Model of Intercultural Sensitivity.* Unpublished Manuscript. Copyright Milton J. Bennett and Janet M. Bennett.

Bermanzohn, Sally Avery. 2003. *Through Survivors' Eyes: From the Sixties to the Greensboro Massacre.* Vanderbilt: Vanderbilt University Press.

Blake, Michael. 2006. "A Part of Me Died in the Iraqi Desert," Iraq Veterans Against the War. Retrieved October 10, 2006 (http:www.ivaw.org/node/243).

Bourdieu, Pierre. 1990. *The Logic of Practice.* Stanford: Stanford University Press.

Braman, Donald. 2004. *Doing Time on the Outside: Incarceration and Family Life in Urban America.* Ann Arbor: University of Michigan Press.

Brooks, Catherine Lynn. 2003. *Walking the Contested Terrain.* MA Thesis, University of Windsor, Canada.

Bruner, J.S. 1987. "Life as Narrative." *Social Research* 54:11–32.

Burke, Martyn. 2011. Producer-Director. *Under Fire: the Psychological Costs of War Reporting.*

Butler, Judith. 2006. *Gender Trouble: Feminism and the Subversion of Identity.* New York: Routledge Press.

Camic, Charles. 1986. "The Matter of Habit." *American Journal of Sociology* 91, 5 (March, 1986), 1039–87.

Caputo, Philip. [1977] 1978. *A Rumor of War.* New York: Ballantine Books.

Cohen, Beth B. 2007. *Case Closed: Holocaust Survivors in Postwar America.* New Brunswick, NJ: Rutgers University Press.

Cohen, Stephen F. 2012. *The Victims Return: Survivors of the Gulag After Stalin.* Exeter, NH: Publishing Works, Inc.

Connor, Jane Marantz and Diane Killian. 2012. *Connecting Across Differences: Finding Common Ground with Anyone, Anywhere, Anytime.* Encinitas, CA: PuddleDancer Press.

Cooney, Guss et al. 2014. "The Unforeseen Costs of Extraordinary Experience." *Psychological Science.* October 1.

Cross, Susan E. and Jonathan S. Gore. 2003 "Cultural Models of the Self," Pp. 536–64 in *Handbook of Self and Identity* edited by Mark R. Leary and June Price Tangney. New York: Guilford Press.

Csikszentmihalyi, Mihaly. 1993. *The Evolving Self.* New York: HarperCollins Publishers, Inc.

Curry, Constance et al., 2000. *Deep in Our Hearts: Nine White Women in the Freedom Movement.* Athens, GA: University of Georgia Press.

Davis, Fred. 1979. *Yearning for Yesterday: a Sociology of Nostalgia.* New York: The Free Press.

DeGruy, Joy. 2005. *Post Traumatic Slave Syndrome: America's Legacy of Enduring Injury and Healing.* Portland, OR: Joy DeGruy Publications, Inc.

Delbo, Charlotte. 1995. *Auschwitz and After.* New Haven: Yale University Press.

Dobie, Katie. 2008. *The Nation.* February 18.

Drain, Lauren, with Lisa Pulitzer. 2013. *Banished: Surviving My Years in the Westboro Baptist Church.* New York: Grand Central Publishing, Hachette Book Group, Inc.

Ebaugh, Helen. 1988. *Becoming an Ex.* Chicago: University of Chicago Press.

Ebert, Roger, 1985. *Sun Times.* September 20.

Erikson, Kai T. 1976. *Everything in its Path: Destruction of Community in the Buffalo Creek Flood.* New York: Simon and Schuster.

Fihla, Nikosinathi B. 2005. *ANC Oral History Project.*

Fink, Sheri. 2009. "The Deadly Choices at Memorial." *ProPublica.* Retrieved May 19, 2015. (www.propublica.org/article/the-deadly-choices-at-memorial-826)

Fleury-Steiner. 2012. *Disposable Heroes: The Betrayal of African American Veterans.* Lanham: Rowman and Littlefield Publishers.

Foucault, Michel. [1967] 1987. "Of Other Spaces, Heterotopias," *Architecture, Mouvement, Continuite* 5:46–49. Retrieved May 19, 2015. (www.foucault.info/documents/heterotoopia/ foucault.heterotopia.en. html)

Frankl, Viktor E. 1963. *Man's Search for Meaning: An Introduction to Logotherapy.* New York: Pocket Books.

Frierson, Cathy A. 2015. *Silence Was Salvation: Child Survivors of Stalin's GTerror and World War II in the Soviet Union.* New Haven: Yale University Press.

Gallagher, Winifred. 2009. *Rapt: Attention and the Focused Life.* New York: The Penguin Press.

Gergen, Kenneth. 1991. *The Saturated Self: Dilemmas of Identity in Contemporary Life.* New York: Basic Books.

Girodo, Michael. 1984. "Entry and Re-Entry Strain in Undercover Agents," Pp. 169–78 in *Role Transitions,* edited by Vernon L. Allen and Evert van de Vliert. New York: Plenum Press.

Glasser, Martin Ira and Robert Krell, eds. 2006. *And Life is Changed Forever.* Detroit: Wayne State University Press.

Goffman, Erving. 1959. *The Presentation of Self in Everyday Life.* New York: Knopf Doubleday Publishing Group.

Goffman, Erving. 1961. *Encounters: Two Studies in the Sociology of Interaction.* Indianapolis: Bobbs-Merrill.

Goffman, Erving. 1963. *Stigma: Notes on the Management of Spoiled Identity.* New York: Prentice Hall.

Goldberg, Denis. 2005. *ANC Oral History Project.* Interviewer: Neo Kgositsile.

Gore, Dayo F., Jeanne Theoharis and Komozi Woodward. 2009. *Want to Start a Revolution? Radical Women in the Black Freedom Struggle.* New York: New York University Press.

Gornick, Vivian. 1977. *The Romance of American Communism.* New York: Basic Books.

Gray, Katti. 2013. "The Run-On Sentence." *The Sun* 451:4–12.

Greensboro Truth and Reconciliation Commission Report, Executive Summary. 2006. Retrieved June 26, 2013. (www.green borotrc.org/exec.summary.pdf.)

Gunaratana, Bhante. 2011. *Mindfulness in Plain English.* Boston: Wisdom Publications.

Hall, Prathia. 2012. "Freedom-Faith," Pp. 172–80 in Holsaert, Faith S. et al., eds, *Hands on the Freedom Plow: Personal Accounts by Women in SNCC.* Urbana: University of Illinois Press.

Hansen, Toran. 2007. "Can Truth Commissions be Effective in the United States? An Analysis of the Effectiveness of the Greensboro Truth and Reconciliation Commission in Greensboro, North Carolina." School of Social Work, University of Minnesota. Retrieved June 16, 2013. (www.cchd.umn.edu/ssw/rjp/resources/RU-dialogue_resources/RJ_Dialogue approaches/Can_Truth_Commissions_Be_Effective_US.pdf)

Harden, Blaine. 2012. *Escape from Camp 14.* London: Penguin Books.

Hartocollis, Anemona. 2013. "Volunteers at Ground Zero Now Face a Demand for Proof." *New York Times.* January 1.

Hedges, Chris. 2002. *War is a Force That Gives Us Meaning.* New York: Public Affairs.

Hedges, Chris. 2010. "Freedom in the Grace of the World." *TruthDig.com.* July 5.

Heidemann, Laura J. 2006. *Recovering from the Revolution: Integrating Guerrilla Ex-Combatants.* MA Thesis. Sociology. University of Wisconsin-Madison.

Heinlein, Sabine. 2013. *Among Murderers: Life After Prison.* Berkeley: University of California Press.

Helmreich, William B. 1992. *Against All Odds: Holocaust Survivors and the Successful Lives They Made in America.* New York: Simon and Schuster.

Herman, Judith Lewis. 1992. *Trauma and Recovery.* New York: Basic Books.

Hill, Jenna Miscavige with Lisa Pulitzer. 2013. *Beyond Belief: My Secret Life Inside Scientology and My Harrowing Escape.* New York: HarperCollins.

Hochschild, Arlie Russell. 1983. *The Managed Heart: Commercialization of Human Feeling.* Berkeley: University of California Press.

Hoffer, Eric. 2002. *The True Believer: Thoughts on the Nature of Mass Movements.* New York: HarperPerennial Modern Classics.

Hoffman, Jan. 2014. "Great Vacation? Don't Brag to Your Friends." *New York Times*. November 6.

Holsaert, Faith S. et al., eds. 2012. *Hands on the Freedom Plow: Personal Accounts by Women in SNCC*. Urbana: University of Illinois Press.

Holstein, James A. and Jaber F. Gubrium. 2000. *The Self We Live By: Narrative Identity in a Postmodern World*. New York: Oxford University Press.

Horowitz, David. 1997. *Radical Son: A Generational Odyssey*. New York: Simon and Schuster.

Hughes, Everett C. 1945. "Dilemmas and Contradictions of Status." *American Journal of Sociology*: 353–59.

Hughes, Rosalie. 2015. "A Crisis of Anxiety Among Aid Workers," *New York Times*, March 8.

Hyde, Judith, Kevin Bales and Marc Levin. 2006. *Physical and Mental Health Aspects of Rehabilitating Children Freed from Slavery*. Washington, DC: Free the Slaves.

Immergut, Matthew. 2014. "A Sociology of No-Self: Applying Buddhist Social Theory to Symbolic Interaction." *Symbolic Interaction* 37 (2):264–82.

Jamail, Dahr. 2009. *The Will to Resist: Soldiers Who Refuse to Fight in Iraq and Afghanistan*. Chicago: Haymarket Books.

Kertesz, Imre. 2004. *Fatelessness*. New York: Vintage International.

Khazan, Olga. 2014, "The Importance of Sharing Experiences." *The Atlantic*. October 16.

Kovic, Ron. 1976. *Born on the Fourth of July*. New York: McGraw-Hill Book Company.

Kovic, Ron. 2005. *Born on the Fourth of July*. New York: Akashik Books.

Langer, Lawrence L. 1995, "Introduction" Pp. ix-xviii in *Auschwitz and After* by Charlotte Delbo. New Haven: Yale University Press.

Lederach, John Paul and Angela Jill Lederach. 2010. *When Blood and Bones Cry Out: Journeys Through the Soundscape of Healing and Reconciliation*. New York: Oxford University Press.

Lee, Spike. Director. 2006. *When the Levees Broke*.

Lembcke, Jerry. 2013. *PTSD: Diagnosis and Identity in Post-empire America*. Lanham, MD: Lexington Books.

Lembcke, Jerry. 1998. *The Spitting Image: Myth, Memory and the Legacy of Vietnam*. New York: New York University Press.

Lerner, Bernice. 2004. *The Triumph of Wounded Souls*. Notre Dame, IN: University of Notre Dame Press.

Levi, Primo. 1985. *Survival in Auschwitz and The Awakening*. New York: Simon and Schuster.

Levi, Primo. 1988. *The Drowned and the Saved*. New York, Simon and Schuster, Inc.

Lewis, Andres B. 2009. *The Shadows of Youth: the Remarkable Journey of the Civil Rights Generation*. New York: Hill and Wang.

Lewis, John with Michael D'Orso. 1998. *Walking with the Wind: A Memoir of the Movement*. New York: Simon and Schuster.

Lifton, Robert Jay. 1963. *Thought Reform and the Psychology of Totalism: A Study of Brainwashing in China*. New York: W.W. Norton & Company.

Lohaus, Dan, Director. 2006. *When I Came Home*.

Luft, Benjamin J., M.D. 2011. *We're Not Leaving: 9/11 Responders Tell Their Stories of Courage, Sacrifice and Renewal*. New York: Greenpoint Press.

Mants, Joanne Christian. 2012. Pp. 128–140 in Holsaert, Faith S. *Hands on the Freedom Plow: Personal Accounts by Women in SNCC*. Urbana: University of Illinois Press.

Maruna, Shadd. 2001. *Making Good: How Ex-Convicts Reform and Rebuild Their Lives*. Washington, DC, American Psychological Association.

Maruna, Shadd, Louise Wilson and Kathryn Curran. 2006. "Why God is So Often Found Behind Bars: Prison Conversions and the Crisis of Self-Narrative." *Research in Human Development* 2 and 3:161–84.

Mathews, Gordon. 2000. *Global Culture/Individual Identity*. New York: Routledge.

Mathews, Kayla. 2014. "Study Suggests 'Extraordinary Experiences' Make You Feel Bad." *Huffington Post*. October 8, December 8. Retrieved July 11, 2015. (www.huffingtonpost.com)

McAdam, Doug. 1988. *Freedom Summer*. New York: Oxford University Press.

McAdams, Dan P. 1997. *The Stories We Live By.* New York: The Guilford Press.

McAdams, Dan P. 2008. *The Person: An Introduction to the Science of Personality Psychology.* Hoboken, NJ: Wiley.

McAdams, Dan P. 2013. *The Redemptive Self: Stories Americans Live By.* New York: Oxford University Press.

Mead, George Herbert. 1934. *Mind, Self and Society.* Chicago: University of Chicago Press.

Davis, Joshua. 2012. "Arab Spring Break." Retrieved May 19, 2015. (www.mensjournal.com/magazine/print.view/arab-spring-break-20120913)

Merton, Robert K. 1957. *Social Theory and Social Structure.* Glencoe IL: The Free Press.

Moorehead, Caroline. 2011. *A Train in Winter.* New York: HarperCollins Publishers.

National Public Radio 2015. "In Northern Ireland, 'Terror Gets Old,' But Divisions Linger." Retrieved July 20, 2015. (www.npr.org)

Nawaz, Maajid with Tom Bromley. 2013. Guilford, CT: Lyons Press.

Nisbett, Richard E. 2003. *The Geography of Thought: How Asians and Westerners Think Differently . . . and Why.* New York: Free Press.

Oberg, Kalvero. 1960. "Cultural Shock: Adjustment to a New Cultural Environment." *Practical Anthropology* 7.

Olson, Gary. 2014. "Want to Prevent PTSD? End Unbridled U.S. Militarism." Retrieved 6/21/2014. (www.commondreams.org)

Omolade, Barbara Jones. 2012. "Building a New World," Pp. 388–94 in Holsaert, Faith S. et al., eds. *Hands on the Freedom Plow: Personal Accounts by Women in SNCC.* Urbana: University of Illinois Press.

O'Neal-McCray. 2012. "Watching, Waiting and Resisting," Pp. 61–66 in Holseaert, Faith S. et al., eds. *Hands on the Freedom Plow: Personal Accounts by Women in SNCC.* Urbana: University of Illinois Press.

Papp, Joseph and Edward R. Pressman, Producers. 1985. *Plenty.*

Parrado, Nanco with Vincent Rause. 2006. *Miracle in the Andes: 72 Days on the Mountain and My Long Trek Home.* New York: Crown Publishers.

Payson, Hope. 2012. Interview, July 26. 2012.

Petersilia, Joan. 2003. *When Prisoners Come Home: Parole and Prisoner Reentry.* New York: Oxford University Press.

Polaris Project. 2012. *Shelter Beds for Human Trafficking Survivors in the United States.*

Polner, Murray. 1971. *No Victory Parades: the Return of the Vietnam Veterans.* New York: Holt, Rinehart and Winston.

Powell, Lawrence N. 2000. *Troubled Memory: Anne Levy, the Holocaust, and David Duke's New Orleans.* Chapel Hill: University of North Carolina Press.

Prochaska, James O., John C. Norcross et al. 1994. *Changing for Good.* New York: Avon Books, Inc.

Rambeau, Janie Culbreth. 2012. "Ripe for the Picking." Pp. 91–100 in Holseart, Faith S. et al., eds. *Hands on the Freedom Plow: Personal Accounts by Women in SNCC.* Urbana: University of Illinois Press.

Rendon, Jim. 2012. "Post-traumatic Stress's Surprisingly Positive Flip Side." *New York Times.* March 25.

Reynolds, John. 2012. *The Fight for Freedom: A Memoir of My Years in the Civil Rights Movement.* Bloomington, IN: AuthorHouse.

Ritzer, George. 2005. *Encyclopedia of Social Theory.* Thousand Oaks, CA: Sage Publications.

Robbins, Tom. 2012. "Judith Clark's Radical Transformation." *New York Times.* January 12.

Rosenberg, Marshall B. and Arun Gandhi. 2003. *Nonviolent Communication: A Language of Life.* Encenitas, CA: PuddleDancer Press.

Rosenberg, Tina. 2012. "For Veterans, a Surge of New Treatments for Trauma." *New York Times.* September 26.

Rudd, Mark., 2009. *Underground: My Life with SDS and the Weathermen.* New York: HarperCollins.

Runningen, Roger. 2013. "Obama Says Mental Health Illness Must Come Out of Shadows." Bloomberg.com. June 3. Retrieved June 30, 2013 (www.bloomberg.com/news/print/2013–06–03/obama-says-u-s-m...)

Salzer, Alicia. 2011. *Back to Life.* New York: HarperCollins.

Saylor, Thomas. 2007. *Long Hard Road: American POWs During World War II.* St. Paul, MN: Minnesota Historical Society.

Schaller, Barry R. 2012. *Veterans on Trial: The Coming Court Battles Over PTSD.* Dulles, VA: Potomac Books.

Schuetz, Alfred. 1944. "The Stranger: An Essay in Social Psychology." *American Journal of Sociology* 49 (6):499–507.

Schur, Edwin. 1971. *Labeling Deviant Behavior.* New York: Harper and Row.

Shapiro, Francine. 2012. *Getting Past Your Past.* New York: Rodale, Inc.

Shepler, Susan. 2014. *Childhood Deployed: Remaking Child Soldiers in Sierra Leone.* New York: New York University Press.

Sherman, Nancy. 2011. *The Untold War: Inside the Hearts, Minds and Souls of Our Soldiers.* New York: W.W. Norton and Company, Inc.

Sherman, Nancy. 2015. *Afterwar: Healing the Moral Wounds of Our Soldiers.* New York: Oxford University Press.

Snow, David A. and Leon Anderson. 1993. *Down on Their Luck.* Berkeley, CA: University of California Press.

Solnit, Rebecca. 2010. *A Paradise Built in Hell: The Extraordinary Communities that Arise in Disaster.* New York: Penguin Books.

Somashekhar, Sandhya. 2013. "Obama Calls for National Conversation about Mental Health. *Washington Post.* June 3.

Stahl, Marion A. 2014. *Anita's Piano: A Story Based on the Life of Anita Ron Schorr.* Corp-Well Publishing.

Stein, Arlene. 2014. *Reluctant Witnesses: Survivors, Their Children, and the Rise of Holocaust Consciousness.* New York: Oxford University Press.

Stets, Jane and Peter J. Burke. 2003. "A Sociological Approach to Self and Identity." Pp. 128–52 in *Handbook of Self and Identity* edited by Mark R. Leary and June Price Tangney. New York: Guilford Press.

Stryker, Sheldon. 1980. *Symbolic Interactionism: A Social Structural Version.* Menlo Park, CA: Benjamin/Cummings.

Svigals et al. 2012. "Collaboration." *Parabola* 37(2):46–59.

Thomson, Ian. 2002. *Primo Levi.* London: Hutchinson.

Tick, Edward. 2005. *War and the Soul: Healing Our Nation's Veterans from Post-traumatic Stress Disorder.* Wheaton, IL: Guest Books.

Turner, R.H. 1976. "The Real Self: From Institution to Impulse." *American Journal of Sociology* 81: 989–1016.

van Gelder, Sarah. 2011. "Can Prison be a Healing Place?" *Yes!* Summer: 38–39.

Viterna, Jocelyn. 2013. *Women in War: The Micro-Processes of Mobilization in El Salvador.* New York: Oxford University Press.

Ward, Colleen and Stephen Bochner et al. 2001. *The Psychology of Culture Shock.* New York: Routledge.

Wasdin, Howard E. and Stephen Templin. 2011. *Seal Team Six: Memoirs of an Elite Navy SEAL Sniper.* New York: St. Martin's Press.

Wessells, Mike. 1977. "Child Soldiers." *Bulletin of the Atomic Scientists.* November/December.

Wessells, Mike. 2006. *Child Soldiers: From Violence to Protection.* Cambridge, MA: Harvard University Press.

Westervelt, Sandra and Kimberly J. Cook. 2012. *Life After Death Row.* New Brunswick, NJ: Rutgers University Press.

Wiesel, Elie, *Night.* 1985. New York: Hill and Wang.

Wills, T.A. 1981. "Downward Comparison Principles in Social Psychology," *Psychological Bulletin* 90 (2).

Wyler, William. 1946. Director. *The Best Years of Our Lives.*

Zeiger, David. 2005. Producer and Director. *Sir! No Sir!*

Index

African National Congress (ANC). *See* political parties and organizations
agency, human, 35, 36, 37, 46, 79–81, 93–94
aid workers. *See* humanitarian aid workers
Alessi, Mark, 38–39, 65, 73, 77, 78, 137
alternative healing practices, 125
American Communist Party. *See* political parties and organizations
anti-apartheid movement. *See* social movements
anti-slavery movement. *See* social movements
anti-war movement. *See* social movements
attention, 102–103
Auschwitz. *See* Holocaust survivors

Beaumont, Andres, 27, 31, 42, 84–85, 137
Beloved Community, 16, 38

challenges of returning to ordinary world, 69–91; as distinct from stages, 70, 142–143; daily life, 74–78; reconstruction of self and identity, 79–84; reinterpreting meaning of extraordinary experience, 84–89; relationships, 89–91; survival, 71–74
child soldiers, xi, xii, xiv, 12–14, 35, 46, 106, 124, 127–129, 131, 134
Civil Rights Movement, 5–6, 15–17, 31, 46, 63–64, 66, 71–73, 74–75, 80–81, 84–86, 88, 96, 98–99, 100, 104, 106–107, 111, 129–130, 134
civil wars, 66–67, 96–97, 120, 127–129
cognitive dissonance, 84
Communist Labor Party. *See* political parties and organizations
Communist Workers Party. *See* political parties and organizations
Communist Party of the Soviet Union. *See* political parties and organizations
concentration camps. *See* Holocaust survivors; resistance, French in World War II
contexts of return, 52–65; ambivalent, 58–61; negative, 54–58; positive, 52–54; family, 61–65; public policy, 65
culture, xi, 4, 6, 8, 11, 12, 14, 15–16, 19, 21, 23–26, 28–31, 33–34, 35–36, 37–38, 41–43, 45, 51, 142
culture shock, 23–24, 25–28, 41

deviance, 140, 141
disaster survivors, xi, 5–6, 19–21, 34, 46, 63, 66, 83, 87, 97–98, 107, 120, 133–134

emotions: emotions management, 36, 81; positive, in extraordinary experiences, 4–5, 21
engulfment, 28, 35, 37–38, 40–41, 82, 83, 109–110; cultural engulfment, 37–38;

role engulfment, 37
ex-identity. *See* role exit
exploratory research, xv, xvii–xviii
extraordinary experiences, as ideal type.
    See ideal type
Eye Movement Desensitization and
    Reprocessing (EMDR), 98, 101

families, 61–65
Farabundo Marti National Liberation Front
    (FMLN). *See* political parties and
    organizations
first responders, 9/11, 52–53

Gardner, Joe, 31, 42, 73–74, 75–76, 84–85,
    91, 137
Greensboro Truth and Community
    Reconciliation Project, 106–107
Gulag, xii, 5, 59–60, 62, 63, 83–84, 86–87,
    90–91, 96, 102, 105–106, 141

habit, 23–25, 41–42, 44–45
happiness. *See* strategies for returning to
    the ordinary world, evaluation
health care, 73–74
Hizab Al-Tahrir. *See* political parties and
    organizations
Holocaust survivors, xi, xiv, xvi,
    xvii–xviii, 5, 6–9, 27–28, 32–33, 34,
    46–47, 53–54, 71, 74, 75–76, 77–78,
    79–81, 88–89, 95–96, 102, 105–106,
    107–108, 113
humanitarian aid workers, xi, xvi, 5, 38,
    65, 73, 77, 78, 120, 121

ideal type, xviii–xix, 3–4, 21, 139–140;
    extraordinary experiences as ideal type,
    4–5, 139–140
identity, xvi–xvii, 4, 23–24, 28–29, 30, 45,
    51; identity salience, 37; narrative
    practices in construction of, 36, 93–94;
    reconstruction of, 79–84; shared,
    40–41; transformation in extraordinary
    experiences, 33–34, 35, 36, 37–41,
    38–40. *See also* self
intelligence agents. *See* undercover agents
intercultural communication, xvi–xvii, 23,
    25–26, 115–116

International Center for Transitional
    Justice (ICTJ), 129–130

journalists. *See* war correspondents

Ku Klux Klan (KKK). *See* political parties
    and organizations

Lerner, John, 40, 137
Lukacs, Eva, 42, 71, 73, 75–76, 78, 80–81,
    88–89, 96, 102, 107–108, 137

marginality, xvi–xvii; constructive and
    negative marginality, 115–116
mass incarceration. *See* prisoners
master status, 37, 82
meaning, xi, 4, 9, 10, 12, 14–16, 18, 19, 21,
    28, 34–35, 37–38, 84–89, 99, 109–110
medical care. *See* health care

needs, human, 24, 35, 36, 45
Nelson, Linda, 33, 42, 87, 111–112, 137
New Left. *See* social movements
non-violent communication (NVC), 131

ordinary world, 141–142

Parallel Universe, 132
peace movement. *See* social movements
political parties and organizations: African
    National Congress (ANC), 40–41, 76;
    American Communist Party, 54–55,
    97–98, 108, 110; Communist Labor
    Party, 99; Communist Party of the
    Soviet Union (CPSU), 59–60, 85–87;
    Communist Workers Party (CWP),
    71–73, 74, 80–81, 88, 134; Farabundo
    Marti National Liberation Front
    (FMLN), 32, 66–67; Hizab Al-Tahrir,
    108–109, 110–111; Ku Klux Klan
    (KKK), 71–73, 74, 88, 96, 107,
    129–130; Weatherman, 76–77, 84–86,
    102–104. *See also* social movements
Post-Traumatic Stress Disorder (PTSD),
    xiv, 43–44, 46–47, 96, 99, 100–101,
    104–106, 121–122, 125–126, 131. *See
    also* trauma
prisoners, xii, xiv, 5, 46, 55–58, 62, 63, 73,
    75, 76, 82–83, 87, 96, 103–104, 105,

109, 119, 120, 121, 122, 123, 127–128, 132–133, 134. *See also* prisoners, exonerated

prisoners, exonerated, 59–61, 75, 83, 89, 95, 96, 104, 120, 121

psychotherapy, 100–102, 104, 115, 121–122, 124, 125–126, 131. *See also* strategies for returning to ordinary world, psychotherapy

public policy, 65, 119–135

purpose. *See* meaning

questions, unanswered, 46–47, 66–67

racism, 56, 73, 97, 113, 121, 134

refugees, 120

religion, as personal healing practice, 102–103

religious groups, xi, xvi, 5, 33, 64–65, 82, 87, 91, 95–96, 111–112, 120, 121, 134

reconciliation, 70, 127, 129–130

research methods, xv–xviii, 137–138

resistance, French in World War II, xii, 58–59, 79–80, 83–84

restoration, 127–129

returnee status, 121

revolutionaries. *See* political parties and organizations; social movements; war veterans

role exit, xvi–xvii, 79–81

Schorr, Anita, 23, 33–34, 36, 71, 73, 74, 76, 77, 79, 80–81, 88–89, 96, 107–108, 137

self, xvi–xvii, 23–24, 28–29, 35, 41, 45; changes in extraordinary experiences, 30–35, 51; false self, 81, 95–96, 113; in recognition of continuity, 109–112; in reconstruction of self and identity, 79–84; levels of cultural self, 29–30; narrative practices in, 36–37, 93–94; presentation of self, 36, 93–94; saturated self, 37; social construction of, 35–37, 142. *See also* challenges of returning to ordinary world, reconstruction of self and identity; identity

significance. *See* meaning

slaves, xi, 5, 71–72, 81–82, 113, 120, 121, 123, 134

Smith, Cameron, 26–27, 31, 75–76, 137

social movements: anti-apartheid, 97; anti-slavery, 71–72, 123; anti-war, 107, 125, 134; New Left, 76–77, 108; student, 76–77, 85–86. *See also* Civil Rights Movement; political parties and organizations; social movements, anti-war; Student Nonviolent Coordinating Committee

spies. *See* undercover agents

stigma, xviii, 37, 60–61, 62–63, 82–83, 96–97, 116, 121–122, 124, 125–126, 127–128

strategies for returning to ordinary world, 93–116; definition, 93, 143; evaluation of, 112–116, 143; nostalgia, 97–99, 114; personal healing practices, 102–103, 115; political action, 105–109, 115–116; psychotherapy, 100–102, 115; recognition of continuity, 109–112, 115–116, 127–128; renewal, 99–100, 114; silence and secrecy, 95–97, 112, 113, 116; support from other returnees, 104–105, 115

student movement. *See* social movements

Student Nonviolent Coordinating Committee (SNCC), 15–17, 18, 98–99, 110–111

survivor mission, 105–106, 115, 120

transition shock. *See* culture shock

trauma, 4–5, 23–24, 41, 42–44, 46–47, 59–61, 81, 88–89, 95, 98, 101, 104, 113, 124. *See also* Post-Traumatic Stress Disorder

traumatic experiences. *See* trauma

undercover agents, xi, xvi, 5, 39–40, 46, 120

veterans. *See* war veterans

war correspondents, xi, 5–6, 14–15, 46, 102, 106, 120

war veterans, xi, xiv, xvi, xvii–xviii, 5–6, 26–27, 31–32, 40–41, 46–47, 58,

66–67, 73–74, 75–76, 79–80, 84–85,
90, 91, 94–96, 97, 99–100, 102,
104–106, 107, 119, 120, 121–122,
125–126, 130, 131, 134, 141
Weatherman. *See* political parties and
organizations

About the Author

Frances V. Moulder earned a B.A. in sociology-anthropology from Wagner College and a Ph.D. in sociology from Columbia University, where she studied with Terence Hopkins and Immanuel Wallerstein as they were developing the world system perspective. While at Columbia, she also studied Chinese language and the cultures of East Asia. She was drawn to the sociological perspective because it illuminated the broad historical and global background of complex social problems and had a tradition of contributing to movements for a better world. Her writing has focused on social issues. She is the author of two previous books, *Japan, China and the Modern World Economy* and *Social Problems of the Modern World: A Reader*. After getting her Ph.D. and beginning a career as a university teacher, she spent a number of years as a community educator and organizer in low income communities. When she returned to higher education, she worked to build bridges between the campus and surrounding communities, both local and global. She was associate professor of sociology at Three Rivers Community College in Connecticut before her retirement and then special lecturer in the Urban and Community Studies Program at the University of Connecticut, Torrington Campus. As a teacher, she supports student fieldwork, internships, and service learning projects, and encourages students to see local conditions and issues in historical and global perspective. She is the recipient of several State of Connecticut Higher Education awards for academic and community service initiatives, which included designing a community research course and programs on intercultural communication.

CPSIA information can be obtained at www.ICGtesting.com
Printed in the USA
BVOW05*2246061115

425499BV00004B/4/P